To my friend and favorite performer, Florence Henderson, who shares my love of God as well as my enjoyment of cooking and feasting—and also for many years has inspired me to "climb every mountain till I find my dream."

Acknowledgments

Many thanks to

Gary Hougen, pastor of the Church of the Incarnation for praying with me for the success of this book.

Past pastors of the Church of the Incarnation: Larry Hilkemann, Jim Reid, Louise Mahan, and Thomas Ostrander.

Our directors of Christian Education—Nancy Bavisotto, Karen Burton, and Gayle Ostrander—for allowing me to share my talents during the summer or provide special programming so that I could enjoy singing with the Incarnation Choir.

My friends who encourage all of my creative endeavors: Carolyn Arnold, Eunice Becker, Diane Blizek, Shane Burton, Ruth Anne Busson, Pat Craig, Cathy Frost, Suzanne Hall, Marge Janovics, Susan Langowski, Nancy Meyer, Carolyn O'Donnell, Kerry Tomb, and Jan Wilson. To the past and present members of the Lincoln Story League, a multitalented group of librarians who share my enthusiasm of story-sharing with children.

To the following libraries for providing exceptional collections and wonderful places in which to work and research: Arlington Heights Memorial Library, Barrington Area Library, Ela Area Library, Indian Trails Public Library, Mount Prospect Public Library, Palatine Area Library, Prospect Heights Public Library, and Schaumburg Public Library.

My devoted dog, Tara's Triumphant Treasure ("Tara"), who reminds me when it's time to play and have fun.

Contents

Introduction

Bible Banquets with Kids is a bounty of biblical programs that can be used with children ages 3 to 11. The 20 programs include a Bible story, creation of a bulletin board, story sharing, creative dramatics, puppetry, games, service projects, music, art projects, and, of course, a meal. A special feature is a memory verse for children to learn. Some programs are designed for children alone, or children and their parents. Others are intergenerational programs in which the children act as hosts of the event, and the entire congregation is invited to participate. Programs are held at church, and make use of the sanctuary, fellowship hall, classrooms, kitchen, and other areas as specified.

The objectives of these programs are to introduce children to Bible teachings and events in an enjoyable, creative manner, while encouraging them to become mission oriented. Each program asks them to bring an offering that will be shared with people within their community. The children are active participants in all of the programs and are called upon to work together and individually. The order of the programs has been used with children successfully for many years, and each program is designed so that the activities lead naturally from one to another. Puzzles that highlight each celebration can be given to children at the conclusion of each program.

As you share these celebrations with children, let the children bask in God's love for them. Let them know that they are created in God's image, that they are good people deserving of God's love. Encourage them through these programs to share God's love with others. Now, celebrate God's love and "eat what is good, and delight yourselves in rich food" (Isaiah 55:2).

HINT ⊙

Bible Banquets with Kids can be used in connection with *Bible Time with Kids* (Abingdon, 1997) and *Worship Time with Kids* (Abingdon, 1998) to plan dynamic, creative programs.

GETTING STARTED

1. Begin planning early, and have all of your materials set out and ready to go *before* the program begins.
2. Visit your public library, parochial school library, and Christian bookstores to find picture books that highlight Bible stories. There are many in publication, and new ones are always being published. Make use of these in your programs.
3. Each program is intended for children ages 3 to 11. Group children together by ages: 3 years to kindergarten; grades 1 and 2; and grades 3 through 5. In smaller churches, divide the children into two groups: 3 years to kindergarten, and grades 1 through 5; or have all ages attend together. Usually the older kids are willing to help younger children. Adapt the program to fit your specific needs and situation.
4. Enlist several adult assistants and meet with them prior to the program, so that they are clear about their responsibilities.
5. Use a variety of storytelling techniques to present the stories. For example: creative dramatics, flannelboards, story cards, reading aloud from well-illustrated books, storytelling with and without props, puppetry, and so forth. Avoid having kids read the story aloud from the Bible, since they find it boring and too much like school.
6. Be aware of any food allergies that children have. Be willing to substitute food, or ask the child's parent/guardian to supply food the child can safely eat.
7. For children who finish an activity early and need to wait for the others to complete their work, set up an area with two cassette players, headphones, Christian children's audiotapes, and books on cassette. Also, provide Bible jigsaw puzzles (wooden, cardboard, or paper-and-pencil), pages copied from Bible coloring books, and picture books. This keeps the children occupied and prevents them from disrupting the others.
8. Have an area where kids can gather to pick up their nametags before the program begins. Play a children's audiotape of Bible songs, and have them sit and listen quietly while they wait for the program to begin.
9. Begin on time. Be fair to those who arrive on time, and begin the program promptly. Avoid recapping or starting over for latecomers.
10. See sections "Room Decoration Ideas" (pages 133-134) and "Discipline Tips" (page 135) for more information.

CHAPTER 1

New Year's Day Parade and Picnic

Invite children and their families to come to a New Year's Day parade and picnic during the month of January. Try holding this celebration on New Year's Day, if enough people are available to attend and assist with the program. Encourage teen and adult musicians to form a "Bethlehem Marching Band."

❏ **Theme:** Celebrating the opportunities and possibilities in the new year that God has given us.

❏ **Memory Verse:** "Therefore, if anyone is in Christ, he is a new creation; the old has gone, the new has come!" (2 Corinthians 5:17 NIV).

❏ **Nametags:** Locate self-adhesive New Year's nametags.

❏ **Food:** Ask individuals or each family unit to bring their own picnic basket filled with picnic goodies. They can eat at tables or on the ground in Bethlehem Square.

❏ **Offering:** Ask every family or child to bring a board book for a new baby. The book can be donated to an organization or agency that works with unwed mothers.

❏ **Time:** 2 to 3 hours.

❏ **Table Decorations:** Provide a variety of brightly colored paper table coverings, plates, napkins, and cups. Place different colors at each table and add streamers and confetti. Wait until it is time to eat before setting up the picnic areas.

❏ **Room Decorations:** Decorate the room to look like the town of Bethlehem as it was when Jesus was born. Place arches over the doors, paint backdrops on shades, and so forth. Set tables up around the walls of the room, leaving a large open space in the middle. This can be called "Bethlehem Square." Use the Sunday school classrooms, since each grade will be working in a different room for a portion of the program.

❏ **Costume Idea:** Dress as Bible characters in the town of Bethlehem. Ask parents to dress their children as the characters from the Bible story they will present.

NEW YEAR'S DAY PARADE AND PICNIC
PROGRAM

Welcome: "It's a New Year" (Sung to "Frere Jacques")

Sing it through several times until everyone knows it, then sing it as a round. End by singing the entire song as a group.

Leader:	It's a new year!
All:	It's a new year!
Leader:	Many possibilities!
All:	Many possibilities!
Leader:	Lots of opportunities!
All:	Lots of opportunities!
Leader:	Let's rejoice!
All:	Let's rejoice!

Welcome everyone and tell them that you are going to celebrate the new year. Talk about all of the opportunities and possibilities God is going to give us in the year to come. Ask, How can we use these opportunities and possibilities to serve the Lord? Explain that you are going to have a New Year's parade in Bethlehem, but first you must make the floats.

Bible Stories: Separate the children into different groups (for example, grade levels, multi-age groupings, and so forth). Choose a different Bible story ("Creation," "Noah's Ark," "Jacob's Ladder," "Jonah and the Whale," "Golden Rule") for each group. You will need one adult per group to share the story with the children.

 Art: Float Making (see page 11)

 Activity: Let's Have a Parade (see page 14)

 Project: Opportunities and Possibilities (see page 14)

 Games: Provide a variety of Bible board games. Encourage people to mingle by filling a solid-colored bowl with different colored paper fish. Place four to six fish of each color in the bowl. Hold the bowl overhead so that people cannot see inside, and ask each person to pull out a fish. Direct everyone with green fish to go to table 1, everyone with blue fish to go to table 2, and so forth.

 Bulletin Board: It's a New Year! (see page 15)

Grace: "Oh, Let's Thank the Lord" (Sung to refrain of "The Battle Hymn of the Republic")

Oh, let's thank the Lord.
For this food that we will eat.
Let's give thanks for the new year, too.
And a great big God bless you!

Picnic: Put the table coverings, plates, napkins, and cups on the floor or tables. Enjoy the picnic.

Closing: "Praaaaaaaise God!" (Let a child lead this.)

Leader:	Praise God for the new year!
All:	Praaaaaaaise the Lord!
Leader:	Praise God for possibilities!
All:	Praaaaaaaise the Lord!
Leader:	Praise God for opportunities!
All:	Praaaaaaaise the Lord!
Leader:	Praise God!
All:	Praaaaaaaise the Lord!

ART: Float Making

CREATION (GENESIS 1-2:3)

Materials: 1 kid's wagon, tissue paper, duct tape and book tape, animal pictures, heavy cardboard, flower-shaped sponges, crayons, glue, scissors, tempera paints (red, yellow, orange, purple, and pink), large silver stars, and flannel board and story figures

Prior to the Program

1. Paint a night sky on a large piece of paper. Let it dry, and attach it to a large piece of cardboard.
2. On another piece of paper paint a blue sky with white clouds and sunshine. Add grassy hills, trees, and flower stems with leaves. Attach this paper to another piece of cardboard.
3. Copy large pictures of animals from kids' coloring books.

Directions

1. Present this story using flannel board.
2. Have kids sponge-paint orange, red, yellow, and purple flowers on the flower stems.
3. Ask the kids to cut a moon from yellow paper and to glue it and the stars to the night sky.
4. Let kids color the animals and glue them to the cardboard scene.

5. Use duct and book tape to attach the scenes to the wagon. The scenes should come down to the bottom of the wagon so that the wheels are almost covered.
6. Choose someone to pull the wagon in the parade.

NOAH'S ARK (GENESIS 6-9)

Materials: wagon, duct tape, large brown cardboard, book tape, animal pictures or puppets, crayons, animal costumes, large sheets of white paper, and flannel board and story figures

Prior to the Program

1. Make two sides of the ark out of heavy brown cardboard or foam core. Cut holes for the windows.

2. Use blue, green, and purple to paint the ocean on the large sheets of white paper. Let them dry, then cut them out to look like waves.

Directions

1. Present this as a flannel board story.
2. Let kids color the animal pictures. Glue the pictures to the back of the windows so that the animals' heads show.
3. Attach the ark to the wagon with duct and book tape. The ark bottom should almost cover the wagon wheels. Tape the waves to the bottom of the ark.
4. Invite a child to be Noah and pull the ark. The other children can portray Noah's family or be in costumes as animals.

JACOB'S LADDER (GENESIS 28:10-22)

Materials: 1 large wooden stepladder on wheels, gold paint, gold cord, Christmas angels, fiberfill, glue

Prior to the Program

Paint the ladder gold and let it dry.

Directions

1. Tell the story to the children without using props or pictures.
2. Have the kids glue the angels to the steps of the ladder. For additional security, use gold cord to tie the the angels to the ladder.
3. Glue the fiberfill to the ladder so that it looks like clouds.
4. Choose a child to portray Jacob and to push the ladder. The other children can dress as angels and walk alongside the ladder.

JONAH AND THE WHALE (JONAH)

Materials: heavy black cardboard or foam core, tempera paints in blues and greens, rhythm instruments, paintbrushes and water, scissors, large sheets of white paper, yarn, underwater cutouts (fish, octopus, starfish, eels, and so forth), glue, Jonah cutouts, crayons, book and duct tape

Prior to the Program

1. Cut two whales out of black cardboard or foam core. Cut a hole for the stomach, then poke a hole in the top of the stomach. (Whale pattern can be found in *Bible Time with Kids*.)
2. Paint the large white pieces of paper to make them look like the ocean. Let dry. Cut the paper in the shape of waves.
3. Cut out a variety of underwater creatures (fish, octopus, starfish, eels, and so forth).
4. Color and cut out two pictures of Jonah. Punch a hole in each and add yarn.

Directions

1. Tell the story to the children.
2. Have one of the kids attach the pictures of Jonah to the whale, so that it looks like Jonah is bouncing around inside the whale's belly.

3. Invite the kids to color the ocean animals and to glue them to the water.
4. Tape the whale to the wagon. Add the waves to the bottom, almost covering the wagon wheels.
5. Choose a child to pull the wagon. Have the other kids form a rhythm marching band.

GOLDEN RULE (MATTHEW 7:12)

Materials: 1 piece of heavy white cardboard or foam core, 1 smaller piece of heavy white cardboard or foam core per child, brushes, gold paint, black marker

Prior to the Program

1. Cut out a large ruler (5 by 2 feet) from the large piece of white cardboard or foam core.

2. Cut smaller rulers (2 feet by 1 foot) from the smaller pieces of white cardboard or foam core.

3. Paint all rulers gold, and let dry. Use black marker to indicate feet and inches on each ruler.

Directions

1. Tell the story and discuss how we can show what the Golden Rule means (for example, helping others, being kind, being honest, and so forth).

2. Give each child a ruler and ask them to think of one thing they can do to live out the Golden Rule. Have them use a black marker to write their sentence on their rulers ("I will be honest," "I will help others," and so forth).

3. Choose one person to carry the Golden Rule. The other children may follow the leader, carrying their rules.

ACTIVITY
Let's Have a Parade

The Lineup: the completed floats, the Bethlehem Marching Band (ask them to play "Onward Christian Soldiers"), dancers, someone dressed as Moses

Lining Up the Parade

Moses leads. The Creation float is next. The children are dressed as animals and people God created. Noah's Ark comes next, then the angels. Jacob's Ladder follows. Jonah and the Whale is the next float. Next comes the Bethlehem Marching Band, then the Golden Rule. The dancers come last.

Directions

1. Have the parade march down the halls and around "Bethlehem Square."
2. Allow each float to take a turn telling its story.

IDEAS ✳

1. Present the parade during the worship service. Let the kids wind their parade up and down the aisles of the sanctuary, with each group stopping to tell their story to the congregation.

2. A simplified version of the idea above is to have the kids make cardboard cutouts of each story and mount them on dowel rods. The kids can then carry the "stories" as they march in the parade.

PROJECT
Opportunities and Possibilities

Materials: 1 empty, clean large glass jar or coffee can per family/individual; 52 Bible verses; card stock paper in a variety of colors; ribbon; sequins; glue; yarn; contact paper in a variety of colors; patterns cut to fit coffee cans, if used (no contact paper is needed if using jars)

Prior to the Program

1. Select 52 Bible verses for participants to learn during the year. Type the list of verses on card stock paper.
2. Make one packet of 52 verses per family/individual.

Directions

1. Explain that everyone is to memorize one Bible verse per week during the coming year, and that prizes will be given to those who do so.
2. Give each family/individual a glass jar or coffee can to decorate and a packet of Bible verses to put inside. Tell them that every Sunday they are to choose a Bible verse, discuss the meaning of the verse, and then memorize it.
3. The following prizes can be given to those who memorize verses.

1 month of verses	—	Bible stickers
2 months of verses	—	Bible pencils
3 months of verses	—	Scripture candies
4 months of verses	—	Bible pins
5 months of verses	—	Special Bible bookmark
6 months of verses	—	Pizza party with the pastor
7 months of verses	—	Paperback book
8 months of verses	—	Cross necklace
9 months of verses	—	Ice cream party with the Christian education director
10 months of verses	—	Choose prize from a treasure box in the pastor's office
11 months of verses	—	Calendar for the following year
Full year of verses	—	Christmas Video Night with the pastor

HINTS ◎

1. Keep an alphabetical as well as Bible order listing of the verses used.

2. Consider making this a Verse of the Month Club rather than a Verse of the Week club.

3. Maintain a list of families/individuals who participate, and of which verses have been memorized.

4. Limit participation in this activity to those who attended the celebration.

BULLETIN BOARD
It's a New Year!

Materials: multicolored paper, letter stencils, stapler, scissors, cloud shapes cut from white paper, brightly colored construction paper in a variety of colors, fine-tip colored markers (red, blue, purple, green)

Prior to the Program
1. Cover the bulletin board with the multicolored paper.
2. Cut the title "It's a New Year!" from the brightly colored construction paper (letters in different colors). Staple the title to the board.
3. Cut from the white paper one cloud per child.

Directions
1. Talk about making New Year's resolutions. Ask the children what they would like to try to do this year.
2. Have the kids write a New Year's resolution and their names on their clouds. Staple the clouds to the bulletin board.

The Bulletin Board

PUZZLE: *A Parade of Love*

Unscramble the words on the floats to discover God's message. Unscramble the word on the sign to learn where you can read this message in the Bible. Decorate the floats.

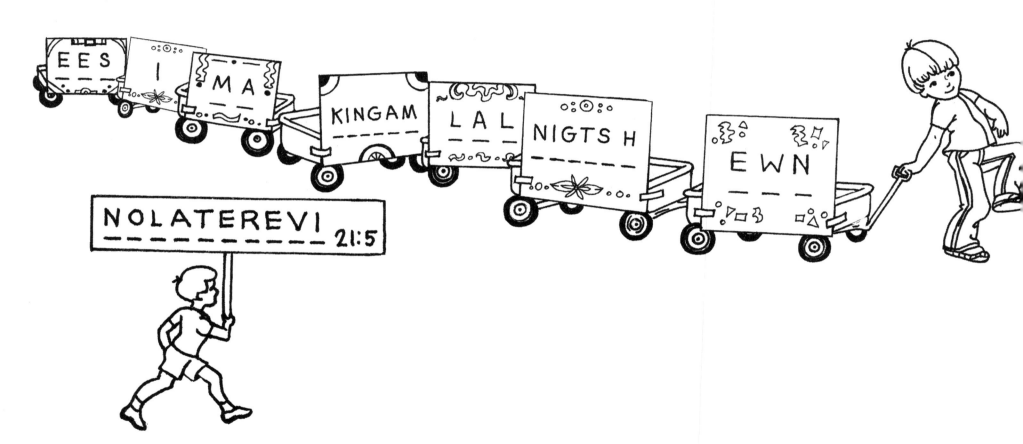

PUZZLE

Where Is the Parade?

Help the kids find their way to the parade!

START

FINISH!

CHAPTER 2

An Epiphany Snack

Epiphany celebrates the arrival of the Wise Men in Bethlehem. We know that the Wise Men brought three gifts (gold, frankincense, and myrrh); however, we do not know exactly how many Wise Men there were. Also, we do not know where they lived or even what route they traveled. These uncertainties provide lots of avenues for creativity in sharing this story.

The Wise Men journeyed about two years before arriving in Bethlehem, which meant that Jesus was an active two-year-old when they met. Here is another opportunity for exploration.

Celebrate this program on Epiphany Sunday and find ways to involve the entire congregation. If your Sunday school meets at the same time as the worship service, consider presenting this program during Sunday school. During the last fifteen minutes of worship, have the Wise Men lead the children into the sanctuary to visit Jesus and his parents in their home. Design the altar to resemble a home in which Jesus would have lived. If your Sunday school meets prior to worship, consider presenting the program during Sunday school. The Wise Men and the children could process into the sanctuary at the beginning of the worship service. After the dramatization and presentation of gifts to Jesus, children can join their parents.

❏ **Theme:** Celebrating the arrival of the Wise Men in Bethlehem.

❏ **Memory Verse:** "On entering the house, they saw the child with Mary his mother; and they knelt down and paid him homage. Then, opening their treasure chests, they offered him gifts of gold, frankincense, and myrrh" (Matthew 2:11).

❏ **Nametags:** Use the crown-shaped pattern on page 21.

❏ **Food:** Crackers (unleavened bread), fruit, and cheese.

❏ **Offering:** Ask each child or family to donate a toy a two-year-old would enjoy. Donate the toys to an agency that provides assistance to families in need.

❏ **Time:** 1 hour.

❏ **Room Decorations:** Paint window shades, depicting the area around city of Bethlehem. Transform the church kitchen into a biblical family home. Use heavy cardboard to create a housefront. Use cardboard cutouts to frame a modern stove so that it looks like an old-fashioned oven. Lower the tables, so that people have to sit on cushions on the floor. In the sanctuary, the altar becomes the home of Jesus and his parents, Mary and Joseph, while the aisles become the streets. Suspend a lighted star of Bethlehem over the altar to recreate the magnificent star that hung over Jesus' home.

❏ **Costume Idea:** Ask everyone in the dramatization to dress in biblical costumes such as simple tunics that tie with cords at the waist. Invite three adult male choir members to portray the Wise Men. Make life-sized cutouts of camels for them. Ask two adults to play the roles of Mary and Joseph. Locate a two-year-old boy or another cooperative child to play the role of Jesus.

AN EPIPHANY SNACK

PROGRAM

Welcome: Have the Wise Men enter the room and greet the children. Act surprised to see the Wise Men appear at Sunday school. Tell them that you are going to learn about their long journey to visit Jesus and about the gifts they brought.

Bible Story: "The Arrival of the Wise Men" (Matthew 2:1-12)
Let the Wise Men tell their story to the children. Each can introduce himself and tell what gift he is going to give Jesus, explaining its meaning. (*Gold* was a gift fit for a king, *frankincense* for a deity, and *myrrh* for someone who was dying.) Ask them to explain that they have not yet visited Jesus, but are stopping to rest on their journey. Have the family (parents and children) "residing" in the "Bethlehem house" in the church kitchen, invite the Wise Men to stay in their home, and serve the men a meal. But first we must make gifts for Jesus.

SOMETHING SPECIAL 🍥

Read to the children *The Christmas Star*, by Marcus Pfister. Let them enjoy the magnificent illustrations.

 Activity: Gifts for Jesus (see page 20)

Song: "We Three Kings of Orient Are"
Ask the three wise men to sing the first and last verses in unison. Each can sing his own verse alone. (Gaspar—gold; Melchoir—frankincense; Balthasar—myrrh) Have them sing as they arrive at the home of Jesus. Teach the children the refrain so that they can sing it as they come into the sanctuary with the wise men.

 Art: Treasure Boxes (see page 21)

Meal: Have the family in the Bethlehem house serve a meal to the Wise Men and all of the people who are outside their house. The family members can ask the Wise Men questions such as "Where are you from?" "Why are you traveling?" and "Where are you hoping to find the baby?"

Procession: "Going to Find Jesus"

Have the wise men thank everyone for their hospitality and prepare to leave.

Balthasar:	Now it is time for us to continue our journey to find Jesus.
Gaspar:	*(to the children)* I have an idea! You can come with us, bring the gifts you created, and give them to Jesus!
Melchoir:	Line up in a straight line behind us and walk quietly. We are going to sing the song again. We will sing the verses, and you can sing the refrain.

The Wise Men lead everyone through the church and into the sanctuary to Jesus' home in Bethlehem, where Joseph and Mary can be playing with Jesus (keeping him occupied, we hope). As soon as the procession enters the sanctuary, begin the first verse of "We Three Kings of Orient Are." Each Wise Man can sing the verse related to his gift as he presents it to Jesus. They can do this a cappella. The children can sing the refrain after each verse. Have the Bethlehem star lit above the altar. The wise men can sing the final verse in unison, with the children singing the refrain. The children can then lay their gifts on the altar as the song is played on the piano/organ.

Balthasar: We must be on our way.
Gaspar: Remember, we must go home another way.
Melchoir: That's right. The angel told us that King Herod is going to try to find Jesus. We will take another way home, so that King Herod does not find out where Jesus lives.

The Wise Men lead the children out of the sanctuary down a different aisle.

ACTIVITY
Gifts for Jesus

Materials: 3 gift patterns per child (each pattern on a separate piece of paper; see page 21 for designs), crayons, pencils, one 12-inch thin ribbon per child, hole punch, shiny gold-and-red wrapping paper, glue

Directions

1. Talk about the gifts that we cannot buy at the store. Ask, What kinds of gifts are these?
2. Copy the gift patterns. Use a variety of colors. Cut out the shapes.
3. Give each child three different gift shapes. Try to make each shape a different color.
4. Let the children use crayons to decorate the front of each gift. Have them write about the three gifts they would give Jesus (one gift per shape).
5. Gather each child's three papers together, punch a hole in the top corner, and tie each set of papers together with ribbon. These gifts will be placed on the altar in church. After church they can be put on the bulletin board for all to enjoy.

6. Use shiny gold Christmas wrapping paper to create a large crown (see pattern on page 21). The size depends on the size of your bulletin board. Use letter stencils to trace the title "Gifts for Jesus" on shiny red paper. Cut out the title and glue it to the crown. Put the crown above the bulletin board.

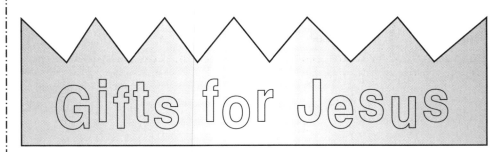

The Bulletin Board

Patterns for the Three Gifts

Crown Pattern

 **ART:** Treasure Boxes

Materials: construction paper; glitter, sequins, shells, jewels, and so forth; crayons; shoe boxes (1 for each child); glue; tempera paints (variety of colors, mixed thick with a few drops of liquid dishwashing soap added); paintbrushes

Prior to the Program
Paint each shoe box a different color (red, blue, purple, brown, or black; orange and yellow do not work well). Let dry overnight.

Directions
1. Give each child a shoe box to decorate with glitter, glue, sequins, shells, jewels, and so forth. Label with each child's name and let dry.
2. Tell the children they can use these boxes for their treasures such as things found on nature walks; cards and notes of love; and photos of family and friends. Invite the children to think of other treasures.

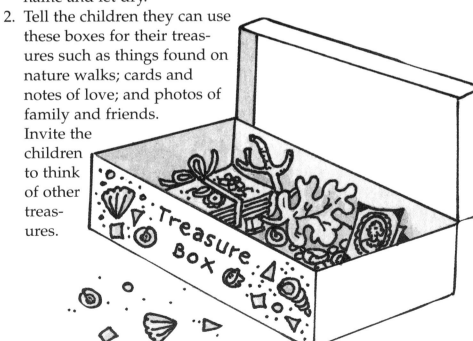

PUZZLE
Where Is Jesus?

Can you help the Wise Men find Jesus?

START

FINISH!

PUZZLE
Message from the Wise Men

Circle the letters where each set of words joins, then unscramble them. What message do they spell?

```
  G                 C                 B                 W
  A                 A                 A                 O
GASPAR            CAMELS              L               WORSHIP
  P                 E                 T                 S
  A                 L               BALTHASAR           H
  R                 S                 A                 I
                                      S                 P
  F                                   A
FIND              GOLD                R       H
  N                 O                         E                 S
  D                 L                         R               STAR
                    D                       HEROD               A
  M                               M           D                 R
MYRRH                             E
  R                               L         FRANKINCENSE
  R                               C         R
  H                               H         A
                                  O         N                   J
                                  I         K                 JESUS
                MELCHOIR                    I                   S
  J                                         N                   U
  O                               L         C                   S
JOURNEY                           O         E
  R                               V         N
  N                             LOVES       S
  E                                         E
  Y
```

CHAPTER 3

Souper Sunday Soup Celebration

❑ **Theme:** Creating a soup meal together

❑ **Memory Verse:** "Use your sickle and reap, for the hour to reap has come, because the harvest of the earth is fully ripe" (Revelation 14:15).

❑ **Nametags:** Choose vegetable shapes from a flannel board book to use as nametags.

❑ **Food:** The soup you will make; ice cream soup; breadsticks; several varieties of crackers; small rye breads; and juice

❑ **Offering:** Ask each child to bring a can of soup to donate to a local food pantry.

❑ **Time:** 2 hours

❑ **Table Decorations:** Plastic vegetables on yellow paper tablecloths

❑ **Room Decorations:** Display soup and vegetable posters on the walls. Paint a backdrop with the Sea of Galilee on it. Have an adult play Jesus. Provide a rowboat where Jesus can sit and teach the story. Provide tables in or near the kitchen where kids can chop vegetables for the soup. Afterward, arrange the tables in a large square, and cover with table coverings and decorations.

This is a great wintertime celebration for children. If desired, hold it on Super Bowl Sunday.

SOUPER SUNDAY SOUP CELEBRATION
PROGRAM

Welcome: Welcome everyone and explain that the program will begin with making a soup that will be eaten later.

 Activity: We're Gonna Make Soup!

Bible Story: "The Parable of the Growing Seed" (Mark 4:26-29)

Materials: A variety of vegetable seeds, pictures of vegetable-producing plants

Talk about how food is planted, grown, and harvested. Explain that God wants us to share the harvest with everyone, and that a portion of the food that God helped us create is being used to make a soup meal that everyone will share. In addition, explain that by bringing cans of soup, we are sharing food with others who do not have enough to eat. Show everyone a variety of vegetable seeds. Talk about how such small seeds grow into large plants that produce vegetables. Use pictures of plants to illustrate how vegetables grow.

 Art: _____'s Soup (see page 25)

 Game: Into the Soup Pot (see page 25)

 Bulletin Board: Praise God for Our Souper Kids! (see page 26)

Grace: Gee Thanks, God! (see page 26).

Meal: Enjoy your meal of "Church-Made Soup," crackers, bread, and juice. For dessert provide a variety of ice cream flavors and let each child choose one or two flavors. Show the kids how to mash and stir the mixture to make ice cream soup. Invite the kids to create a chant about making ice cream soup.

 **ACTIVITY**
We're Gonna Make Soup!

SOMETHING SPECIAL 🎀

Share any of these stories:
Group Soup by Barbara Brenner
Uncle Willie and the Soup Kitchen by DyAnne DiSalvo-Ryan
Growing Vegetable Soup by Lois Ehlert
Button Soup by Doris Orgel

Materials: several large soup cooking pots; whole bay leaves; water (16 to 20 cups per pot); baby wipes; vegetable peeler; meat-cutting scissors; 1 large plastic bowl per pot of soup to be made; bouillon cubes (1 small cube per cup of water); vegetables per pot (4 carrots, 4 celery stalks, 4 red potatoes, 1 small onion, 1 large baking potato); 2 cups of rice or alphabet noodles per pot; 2 boned and skinned chicken breasts per pot, cut into chunks; parsley; knives; 1 cutting board per vegetable and meat table; measuring cup at rice/noodles table; 1 soup bowl, napkin, cup, and soup spoon per person

Prior to the Program

1. Set up the tables in the shape of a square. In the center of the square, place another table for the pots of water with bouillon cubes.

2. Wash the carrots, celery, potatoes, and chicken. Peel the carrots, and trim the excess fat from the chicken.

3. Boil the water with the bouillon cubes. Add chopped onion and parsley for flavoring. The water will need to be hot when veggies are added.

Directions

1. Divide the children into groups of three or four per pot of soup

to be made. Let the older kids chop the vegetables, and the younger kids put the veggies into the bowl. In addition, the younger children can crunch up the bay leaves. Have the kids say the rap "We're Gonna Make Soup!" like a chant as they cut the vegetables.

2. After all of the ingredients have been chopped and put in the bowl, ask an adult to put the ingredients into the pots of boiling water. Simmer at least one hour.

WE'RE GONNA MAKE SOUP!

Refrain:
We're gonna make soup!
We're gonna make soup!
We're gonna make soup . . . together!

Verse:
Chop up the carrots! Chop up the carrots!
Chop up the carrots . . . and put 'em in the bowl!

Change the verse as each vegetable or meat is added to the bowl (saying "celery," "potatoes," "chicken," and so forth). Add, "Crunch up the bay leaves . . . and put 'em in the bowl!" after all the vegetables have been added. Repeat the refrain after each verse. Encourage kids to clap, snap, tap feet, and move to the rhythm of the chant when they are not busy chopping.

Now let's grab the noodles!
Now let's grab the noodles!
Now let's grab the noodles . . . and dump 'em in the bowl!
REFRAIN

ART

_____'s Soup

Materials: one 11-by-18-inch piece of white construction paper per child; crayons; pencils

Directions

1. Have each child print "_____'s (his or her name) Soup" across the top of the piece of paper.
2. Invite each child to make up his or her own soup recipe. They can choose what ingredients to put in it and how it should be cooked (temperature, how long, and so forth).
3. Have the children draw pictures of their soup.

Barbara's Chocolate Soup

Ingredients:	1. Mush up ice cream into soup.
Chocolate ice cream	2. Add Kisses, M & M's and Heath Bars.
Chocolate Kisses	
M & M's	3. Mix it all up.
Crunched up Heath Bars	4. Share it with a friend!

GAME
Into the Soup Pot

Materials: laminated pictures of vegetables (about 12 by 12 inches), 1 per child; cassette player and audiocassette of children's songs; soup pot large enough to hold all of the children (Block off a section of the room as the "soup pot.")

Directions

1. Tape the pictures of vegetables to the floor. Have each child find a vegetable to stand on.
2. Play the cassette tape as the children walk around the room.

---

3. When the tape is stopped, everyone must find a vegetable to stand on. Before starting the music again remove one veggie.
4. Play the tape as the kids walk around. Stop the tape. This time one person will be without a vegetable, and that child will go into the "soup pot." Before starting the music remove another veggie. Keep playing until all the kids are in the soup pot.
5. As children go into the soup pot, hand them a veggie picture. Have another adult with a big spoon "stir the pot of vegetable soup." The kids can move and dance around inside the pot. Let the kids make up a chant or a rhyme about being in the pot of soup.

BULLETIN BOARD
Praise God for Our Souper Kids!

Materials: red, black, and white construction paper; yellow chalk or crayons; scissors; stapler; letter stencils

Prior to the Program

1. Cover the bulletin board with red construction paper.
2. Make a large soup bowl from white paper. Use letter stencils to trace the words "Praise God for Our Souper Kids!" onto black construction paper. Cut them out and glue them to the front of the bowl.

The Bulletin Board

3. Use yellow crayons or chalk to color the inside of the bowl, so that it looks like chicken broth swirling around. Put the soup bowl on the bulletin board.
4. Complete the bulletin board with one of the following options:
   • Take an instant photo of each child, or ask them to bring a wallet-sized school photo to the program. Ask each child to staple his or her photo inside the bowl of soup.
   • Give each child a piece of paper with a name other than his or her own on it. Let the kids write an affirmation about the child whose name is on their slip of paper, and place the slips in the bowl.
   • Attach the affirmations to the photos and put them in the bowl.

GRACE: Gee Thanks, God!

Materials: 1 large soup pot, plastic vegetables (carrots, celery, onion, turnips, potatoes, and so forth), plastic pieces of chicken, real noodles/rice

Directions

1. Choose several children to be the "cooks." The others may assist by clapping their hands and stamping their feet.
2. Give each cook a vegetable, a piece of chicken, or a cup of rice/noodles.
3. One at a time, each cook will add something to the pot. As ingredients are added say this rap (repeat it, substituting each food until everything is in the pot):

God created carrots! God created carrots!
God created carrots! For us to eat!
Gee thanks, GOD!

End by saying:

Gee thanks, God!
Gee thanks, God! Thanks, God!
Thanks, God!
Geeeeeeeeeeeeeeeeeeeee thanks, God!

HINT

Substitute picture cards of each ingredient. Look for them in teacher supply stores and catalogs, or create your own from flannel board pattern books. Trace, color, and cut the patterns out. Glue them to large pieces of paper, and cover with clear contact paper.

PUZZLE

Soup's On!

Unscramble these ingredients that we put in soup.
Print them in the proper spaces inside the bowl of soup.
The circled letters spell a message.

LIONBULO BUCES   TAWER   LOODNES
VESLEA YAB   ROTCARS   KENCHIC
TOPATOES   YRELEC   SONION

PUZZLE

Alphabet Soup

Color the *Y*s yellow and the *O*s orange.
What do the alphabet letters spell?
Print your name on the bowl and color it.

CHAPTER 4

A Friendship Food Faire

This is a good program for February, and can be held in connection with Valentine's Day. Ask each child to bring a friend.

❏ **Theme:** Friendship

❏ **Memory Verse:** "Dear friends, let us love one another, for love comes from God" (1 John 4:7a NIV).

❏ **Nametags:** Use self-stick nametags.

❏ **Food:** A variety of sandwich fixings; chips; lemonade; and "friendship cupcakes"

❏ **Offering:** Ask each child to bring a children's book, which will be donated to a church that has been damaged or destroyed by a disaster. The books should feature a Christian theme and be suitable for a church library.

❏ **Time:** 1½ to 2 hours

❏ **Room Decorations:** Decorate the room with a variety of hearts. Inside each heart place a picture of Jesus, the disciples, or other Bible characters. Provide tables where the children can work on art projects and eat. Use Valentine's Day table coverings, plates, cups, and napkins. Provide an open area for games.

A FRIENDSHIP FOOD FAIRE

PROGRAM

Welcome: Welcome the kids and tell them you are going to celebrate the gifts of friendship.

Bible Stories: Ask the children to share their thoughts on friendship and on what makes a good friend. Tell them that Jesus wants to be our friend, and that he will help us if we let him. Talk about Jesus' friendship with his twelve disciples. Share the stories about Jesus calming the storm and walking on water. Ask, Why did Jesus do this for the disciples? (Because he loved them and wanted to show them how friends help one another.) Invite the children to share their thoughts and feelings on other stories where Jesus showed friendship toward people (the Lord's Prayer, the washing of his disciples' feet, the Last Supper, and so forth). Explain that God sent Jesus to be our friend and to show us how to live. God wanted Jesus to teach lessons about love and friendship. Ask the children what their friends do to help them, and how they help their friends.

Song: "What a Friend We Have in Jesus"

 Activity: Friendship Cupcakes (see page 30)

 Game: Balloon Pop (see page 30)

 Art: Friendship Cards (see page 31)

Activity: Friendship Cheer (see page 31)

Bulletin Board: What a Friend We Have in Jesus (see page 32)

Grace: "Jesus Is My Friend" (Teach it to the children, then say it together.)

Jesus is my friend,
And yours too!
Jesus stays with us
In all we do!
Let us thank God for our food,
And promise to do
Everything that's good!

Meal: Arrange the sandwich fixings on a large table and let the kids create their own sandwiches. Provide chips, drinks, and a friendship cupcake for each child (see page 30).

Closing: "Thank You, Jesus" (Do it as a rap. Alternate clapping and snapping.)

Thank you, Jesus, for bein' our friend.
Thank you, Jesus, for givin' us love.
Thanks for teachin' us how to live.
Thanks for bein' willin' to forgive!
Help us, Jesus, to follow your way!
Help us each and every day!

> ## SOMETHING SPECIAL
>
> **Read one or more of these stories as you wait for the heart prints to dry:**
>
> *Christina Katerina and Fats and the Neighborhood War* by Patricia Lee Gauch
>
> *Andrew Jessup* by Nette Hilton
>
> *The Rainbow Fish* by Marcus Pfister
>
> *Rainbow Fish to the Rescue* by Marcus Pfister

ACTIVITY
Friendship Cupcakes

GAME
Balloon Pop

Materials: white and pink cake mixes (enough to make 6 cupcakes per child); heart-shaped cupcake tins; mixers; pink frosting; ovens; red and pink decorating gels; wooden spoons; red and pink sprinkles; paper heart-shaped cupcake holders; ingredients listed on the box of cupcake mix

Prior to the Program
Assemble the ingredients so that each group can measure and mix them for the cupcakes.

Directions
1. Divide the children into groups of three to four people. Let each group measure and mix the ingredients to make the cupcake batter.
2. Let each child spoon batter into six heart-shaped cupcake tins.
3. Bake the cupcakes according to the directions.
4. Allow the cupcakes to cool before frosting and decorating with gels.

HINT

1. Ask one or two adults to bake the cupcakes while you continue with the program.
2. Label each child's cupcakes before putting them in the oven, so that when the cupcakes cool, the children get to decorate their own.
3. Plan to make several dozen cupcakes. Bake enough so that each child can eat one cupcake at the meal, take two home, and share three with members of the church staff. Place cupcakes for the staff in an air-tight container and deliver them to the church office with a note saying that they are from the children.
4. Consider baking a few cupcakes prior to the program and letting the kids decorate them.

Materials: large red and pink balloons (3 per child, with several extras in case of accidental popping); audiocassette player and a tape of lively Christian songs; red felt pens; small strips of paper; fun inexpensive prizes (stickers, bookmarks, temporary tattoos, and so forth)

Prior to the Program
1. Write a variety of actions on the slips of paper.
   —Sing the song "Make New Friends" to win a prize.
   —Recite the following Bible verse _____ (choose one from a list the kids have memorized) and receive a prize.
   —Tell us the name of your Savior and win a prize.
   —Answer this question and receive a prize (have a list of age-appropriate questions to ask each child who gets this).
2. Insert the slips of paper into balloons. Blow up the balloons and tie the ends. Store the balloons in large plastic garbage bags until it is time for the game.

Directions
1. Put the balloons in the middle of the open area.
2. When the music plays, the kids are to walk around the room among the balloons. When the music stops, they should grab a balloon and pop it (by sitting on it, stomping on it, and so forth).
3. When the slip of paper comes out, the kids must do what it says to get a prize.
4. Keep playing until all of the balloons are gone. Plan to play three rounds.

ART: Friendship Cards

Materials: 1 sheet of sandpaper per child; red crayons; 5 to 10 pieces of white or light pink card stock paper per child; hot irons and ironing boards (1 adult or teenager at each ironing station); large food storage bags; 1 lightweight towel per iron

Directions
1. Have each child draw a design on a piece of sandpaper, using a red crayon. Have the kids press hard with the crayons. Be prepared to help them by going over their strokes. If older kids choose to write words, they must write them backwards so that the letters will appear correctly on the note cards. For example, "love" would be printed as "EVOL."

EVOL

2. Give each child 5 to 10 sheets of white or pink card stock paper. Let the children decide how to fold them to accommodate the sandpaper.

3. Ask children to come one at a time to one of the ironing boards, where the adult or teen will help them make their prints.

4. Lay the card stock on the ironing board. Place the sandpaper on top, with the sandpaper side down. Place a lightweight towel on the back of the sandpaper and iron it a few seconds. Remove the iron, wait a few seconds, then remove the towel and sandpaper to reveal the print. Let it cool.

5. Slip each child's note cards into a plastic food storage bag, close it, and label it with the child's name. Kids can give these to their parents as gifts.

ACTIVITY
Friendship Cheer

Materials: 7 pieces of white paper (12 inches square), 7 pieces of white card stock paper (12 inches square), pencils, black markers, bright colored crayons, letter stencils, rubber cement, clear contact paper, large white envelope

Prior to the Program
1. Use the letter stencils to trace one letter of the word "friends" on each piece of white paper. Use crayons to color in the letters.
2. Use rubber cement to glue the white papers with the letters onto the white pieces of card stock paper.
3. Cover them with clear contact paper. Store them in the envelope.

Directions

1. Choose seven children to be "cheer leaders." Have them stand in a horizontal line facing the "cheering section." Show them how to hold the cards facedown, so that the "cheering section" cannot see the letters. When the kids flip the cards up, the cards should be right side up.

2. Choose one child to be the Announcer. Now you are ready for the cheer.

Announcer:	Give us an *F*!
Child 1:	*F! (Holds card high)*
Others:	*F!*
Announcer:	Give us an *R*!
Child 2:	*R! (Holds card high)*
Others:	*R!*
Announcer:	Give us an *I*!
Child 3:	*I! (Holds card high)*
Others:	*I!*
Announcer:	Give us an *E*!
Child 4:	*E! (Holds card high)*
Others:	*E!*
Announcer:	Give us an *N*!
Child 5:	*N! (Holds card high)*
Others:	*N!*
Announcer:	Give us a *D*!
Child 6:	*D! (Holds card high)*
Others:	*D!*
Announcer:	Give us an *S*!
Child 7:	*S! (Holds card high)*
Others:	*S!*
Announcer:	What does it spell?
All:	*Friends!*
Announcer:	What do friends do?

Now the fun starts. Let the kids yell out what friends do for one another (play, help, care for, teach, and so forth). See what the kids come up with. Then repeat the beginning sequence.

BULLETIN BOARD
What a Friend We Have in Jesus

Materials: large bulletin board; letter stencils; large heart-shaped cookie cutters; shiny red package wrapping paper; powdered red tempera paint; scissors; red markers; pencils; stapler; white paper to cover bulletin board; disposable pie tins

Prior to the Program

1. Trace the letters of the title—"What a Friend We Have in Jesus"—onto the shiny, red paper. Cut them out and glue them to the white background.

2. Mix the powered red tempera until it is thick. Divide it into several pie tins.

Directions

The Bulletin Board

1. Lay the white paper flat on a large table. One at a time, let each child dip the cookie cutter into the paint and press the cutter to the white paper to make a heart-shaped print. (Do not move the cutter around; press it down, and lift it up.)

2. While the paint is drying, read a story about friendship. Ask, How can we be good friends? (By helping, caring, sharing, and so forth.) Invite the children to use the red markers to write their one-word thoughts inside the heart-shaped prints.

3. Put the paper on the bulletin board.

PUZZLE
It All Adds Up

Add the numbers inside the hearts. Use the chart to decode the words. Then put the words in the correct order.

A=1	E=5	I=9	M=13	Q=17	U=21	Y=25
B=2	F=6	J=10	N=14	R=18	V=22	Z=26
C=3	G=7	K=11	O=15	S=19	W=23	
D=4	H=8	L=12	P=16	T=20	X=24	

10+11= 12+7=

5+7= 9+6= 11+11= 3+2=

10+5= 11+3= 5+0=

0+4= 4+1= 1+0= 8+10=

2+4= 9+9= 5+4= 2+3= 6+8= 1+3= 10+9=

0+1= 7+7= 8+7= 10+10= 4+4= 1+4= 9+9=

6+6= 0+5= 18+2=

PUZZLE
God's Love

Connect the dots. Color the Rs red and the Ps pink.

CHAPTER 5

Fabulous Fishes-and-Loaves Lunch

This program can be used any time of the year, but makes a great springtime program in March. Consider asking members of your Confirmation class to help with the program as a part of their church service project. Or perhaps your junior and senior high students can help. This is a good way to involve youth in a different aspect of your Christian education program.

- ❑ **Theme:** Sharing with those less fortunate
- ❑ **Memory Verse:** "They all ate and were satisfied" (Mark 6:42 NIV).
- ❑ **Nametags:** Use the pattern on page 36 to make fish-shaped nametags. Print each child's first and last name on both sides of the tag. Punch a hole in the top and thread with yarn so that the tag slips over the child's head.
- ❑ **Food:** Fish sticks, bread, grapes, fish-shaped crackers, cookies, and juice
- ❑ **Offering:** Ask each child or family to donate one nondisposable lunch sack packed with items such as a juice box, a package of cookies, a small bag of chips, a package of crackers, and a box of raisins. Donate the lunch sacks to a local food pantry. Use large plastic laundry baskets to collect the lunches.
- ❑ **Table Decorations:** Provide large fish-shaped place mats in a variety of colors. Use a small fish bowl with a live goldfish as the centerpiece.
- ❑ **Costume Idea:** Ask people to dress in costumes as Jesus and the disciples.
- ❑ **Room Decorations:** Use fish nets filled with plastic fish. Locate a rowboat with oars and drape it with a fish net. Glue blue, plastic food wrap to a large sheet of blue paper so that it resembles the Sea of Galilee. On a window shade, paint a grassy area with mountains behind it. Place artificial grass on the floor, and add a large rock or tree stump for Jesus to sit on. You will need an open area for games, and tables for art projects and meals.

FABULOUS FISHES-AND-LOAVES LUNCH

PROGRAM

Enlarge the pattern on page 36 and give each child a large fish place mat to color as they wait for the program to begin. Have them put their name on it so that they can use their own place mat during the meal.

Welcome: Welcome everyone by saying that you are going to have a fabulous fishes-and-loaves lunch just like the people had in Jesus' time.

Leader: Let us praise God for his many blessings!
Children: We give thanks to the Lord!

Song: "Praise the Lord!" (Sung to "Mary Had a Little Lamb")

Praise the Lord and clap your hands,
Tap your toes, stamp your feet!
Praise the Lord and jump up high!
Let's praise God together!

Encourage the children to think of movements. Simplify this for a young age group.

 Activity: A Picnic Basket of Prayers (see page 36)

Story: "I'll Share Mine with You" (see page 36)

 Game: Let's Go Fishing (see page 37)

 Art: Favorite Foods (see page 38)

Sharing Our Gifts: Pass the basket around the group, and have the children place their lunch sacks inside. Several baskets may be needed, depending on the size of your group and the number of lunch sacks collected. Play a tape of calming instrumental music while the basket is being passed.

Sing: "We Come to Give" (Sung to "When the Saints Go Marching In")

We come to give! (*Clap, clap, clap, clap*)
Our gifts to God! (*Clap, clap, clap, clap*)
We come to give our gifts to God!
Please share them with the others!
We come to give our gifts to God!

Bible Story: "Jesus Feeds the Multitudes" (adapted from John 6:1-15). See page 38.

Grace: "Oh, Bless This Food" (Sung to "When the Saints Go Marching In")

Oh, bless this food! (*Clap, clap, clap, clap*)
That we share! (*Clap, clap, clap, clap*)
Oh, bless this food we share together!
We give thanks for all our blessings!
Oh, bless this food we share today!

Enjoy the Feast: Ask the children to stay in their groups and enjoy the feast.

Closing: "Let Us Remember to Share" (Ask a child to lead this.)

Let us remember to share our gifts with those who are in need.

Nametag and Pattern

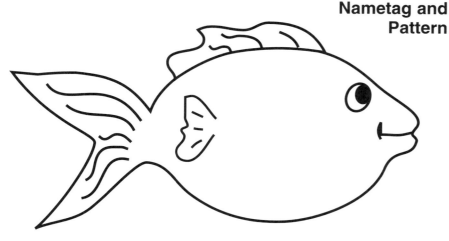

ACTIVITY
A Picnic Basket of Prayers

Materials: 1 picnic basket, 1 paper plate per child, crayons, pencils

Directions

1. Ask each child to write an original prayer on the front of the paper plate and to draw a picture of their prayer on the back.

2. Sit on the floor in a circle. Pass the picnic basket around the circle. Let each child share the prayer, show the plate, and then put it inside the basket.

STORY
I'll Share Mine with You

Scripture: "Truly I tell you, just as you did it to one of the least of these who are members of my family, you did it to me" (Matthew 25:40).

Materials: 1 sack lunch consisting of a peanut butter and jelly sandwich; chips; cheese; carrots; celery; and an orange cut in half; a tin of chocolate chip cookies

Six adults or older youth will be needed as helpers.

Sit on a chair, with the children gathered on the floor in front of you. Take out your lunch and start to eat it. Helper 1 enters, sits next to you and stares at your food.

HINT ⊙

Practice this with the helpers before sharing the story with the children.

You:	Do you need something?
Helper 1:	No, I'm just hungry. I didn't have any breakfast this morning.
You:	Would you like to share my lunch? (*Offer person half of sandwich*)
Helper 1:	Thank you! (*Takes sandwich and begins to eat*)

Helper 2 enters, sits down on the other side of you and stares at your food.

Helper 2:	Boy does that look good! I forgot my lunch at home. It's going to be a long wait until dinner.
You:	I have an orange you can have. (*Gives orange to Helper 2*)
Helper 2:	Thanks! (*Takes orange and eats it*)

Continue in this manner until everything except the chocolate chip cookies are gone. Have each helper share a different reason for not having lunch ("Someone stole it"; "We ran out of money this week, so I have to go without lunch"; and so forth.) Carry on a conversation with the helpers as you are eating with them.

Helper 6: Hi, everyone! What are you doing?

All: Eating! Having lunch. _____'s being real nice and sharing her *[or his]* lunch with us!

Helper 6: Oh, I don't have any lunch today, and I'm starving.

You: Oh no, if you think I'm going to share these home-baked chocolate chip cookies, you're wrong! I'm eating all of them myself.

The reaction from the children will be interesting.

You: What's wrong? Do you really think I should share my chocolate chip cookies?

Let the kids respond.

Helper 1: Isn't that what Jesus would want you to do? You've shared the rest of your lunch. I think you should be nice and share the cookies, too.

Think it over.

You: You're right. Jesus would want me to share the cookies.

Give Helper 6 some cookies and share the rest with the others in the group.

You: Well, I just happen to have a big tin of home-baked chocolate chip cookies to share with each of you. *(Give one to each child)*

GAME: *Let's Go Fishing*

(Let Jesus lead this. This creates the bulletin board.)

Materials: large bulletin board; a sign that reads "Fishing for Jesus!"; an animal-shaped, child-sized swimming pool or large baby bath; fish pattern on page 36; 2 colored, construction-paper fish per child; 1 magnet-attracting paper clip per child; a long dowel rod with a 36-inch string attached; a magnet attached to the end of the string on the dowel rod; a large piece of fish net; blue plastic food wrap; white construction paper; stapler; 1 clothespin per child, colored markers

Prior to the Program

1. Create the "Fishing for Jesus!" sign using the colored markers and white paper. Attach it to the board.
2. Label the construction-paper fish with words such as "helping," "caring," "love," "peacemaking," "sharing," and "teaching." Make two identical fish for each word. Put a magnet-attracting paper clip on one set of fish.
3. Put one of each fish into the "pond," word side down. Keep the duplicates separate.
4. Cover the board with blue paper. Cover the paper with blue food wrap so that it looks like water. Attach the fish net to the board. Clip the clothespins to the net.

Directions

1. Let each child take turns dropping the fishline into the fish pond. When a fish is caught, have the child take the fish off the hook and read what is on the back, saying, "I caught some _____ (love, helping, kindness, and so forth)!" Give the child the fish that is identical.
2. Play until all fish have been caught and every child has a set of two fish.

3. Discuss the meaning of the words that were caught. Ask, How can you be more caring this week? ("I can help take care of my little sister." "I can send a card to my grandma.") How can you be more helpful this week? ("I can help my friend Lisa with her math." "I can help Mom fix dinner." and so forth.) Help the children identify specific ways they can achieve their "goal" for the coming week, and write their sentences on both fish.

4. Use clothespins to attach one fish to the fish net. Invite the kids to take the other fish home as a reminder of their intention for the coming week. The following week, ask the children and their parents how they did with their "goals." Encourage them to make their actions a habit.

The Bulletin Board

Help younger children by writing their sentences for them.

ART: Favorite Foods

Materials: 1 large white heavy-duty paper plate per child, crayons, pencils

Directions

1. Let each child draw a picture of his or her favorite foods on the front of the plate.

2. Invite the children to write about their choice on the back of the plate. Also, ask them to write about how they can share food with people who do not have enough to eat.

BIBLE STORY
Dramatization: Jesus Feeds the Multitudes

Materials: 1 small basket per child; items to go inside the baskets (large bunch of grapes, cheese, cookies, carrots, celery, and other items except the bread and fish); bread; fish sticks; 1 large container of lemonade or fruit juice per group; colored napkins or ribbons; 2 larger baskets (one for the fish, and one for the bread) per group

Prior to the Program

1. Divide the children into groups of four or five, with one disciple (youth or adult) per group. Place a basket of grapes, a bas-

ket of cheese, a basket of cookies, a basket of veggies, and a large container of juice among each group. Each child in the group will carry a different item. This will allow the children to share what they have when it is time for the feast.

2. Color code the baskets by tying colored ribbons on the handles or by lining the baskets with colored napkins. For example, there might be one set of baskets with green ribbons or napkins, and another set with yellow ribbons or napkins, and so forth. This will allow you to divide the kids into groups that will eat together.

3. Heat the fish sticks. They should be hot and ready to serve when the time comes. Have people working in the kitchen during the program. They can put the fish sticks into baskets. Each group will get one basket of fish sticks and one basket of bread.

4. Ask several adults or older youth to help with this activity. One can portray Jesus, and the others the disciples. An older elementary child can portray the little boy who shares his lunch, and the children can portray the multitudes.

Directions

1. Give each child a basket or a jug of juice to carry.
2. Have the youth playing the disciples, the child playing the child who shares his lunch, and Jesus dramatize what happened.
3. To execute the fishes and loaves multiplying, have two baskets. Line the bottom of each with either a bunch of fish sticks or bread. Cover both with a large napkin or cloth. Lay two fish sticks on top of the napkin or cloth in the fish basket and five pieces of bread on top of the bread basket. Have the disciples give the baskets to Jesus. Taking one basket at a time, Jesus will turn so that the group cannot see him, and remove the cloth to uncover the bread. Next, he will remove the cloth covering the fish and there will be more fish sticks.

HINTS

1. Prepare a sign-up sheet for the program, and divide the children into groups beforehand. This avoids hurt feelings and someone feeling "left out." Color code the groups by using colored nametags (that is, blue nametags for the blue group, and so forth). Print the children's names on the nametags prior to the program.
2. Practice the dramatization with "Jesus and the disciples" prior to the program.

4. Continue with the story. Have the disciples lead each group to a separate area of the room for the meal. The group with the green baskets will sit in one area, those with blue baskets in another area, and so forth. Each group will sit in a circle on the floor.

5. The disciples will distribute one basket of bread and one basket of fish sticks to each group.

6. Share the grace (see page 35) and enjoy the feast. Help the kids decide how to share the items in each of their baskets.

While they are in their groups, have each disciple lead a discussion. Ask the children, How did this happen? Was it a magic trick? How do you think they had enough food to feed all those people and still have food left over? How did the disciples feel when Jesus told them to feed the people? Why? How would you feel if Jesus asked you to do this? Explain that when God created the world, God made sure that there would be enough food for everyone. Ask, How can we help those who do not have enough to eat? What does Jesus want us to do to help those who do not have enough to eat? What did you bring today that will help others get enough to eat?

PUZZLE
More Than Enough

When they started, they only had two fish and five loaves of bread. They managed to feed over 5,000 people with them. How did they come to have more than enough food to feed all those people?
Unscramble the words and print the letters in the blanks. The circled letters spell out the message.

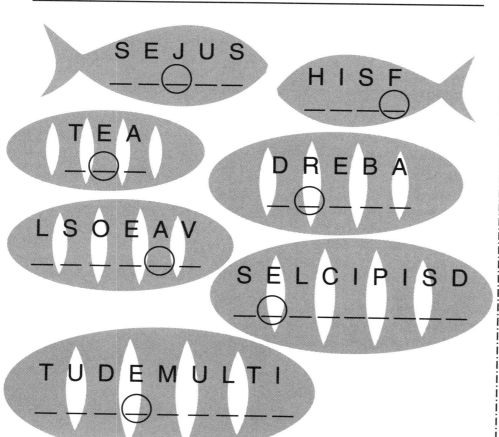

S E J U S
_ _ Ⓞ _ _

H I S F
_ _ _ Ⓞ

T E A
_ Ⓞ _

D R E B A
_ Ⓞ _ _ _

L S O E A V
_ _ _ _ Ⓞ _

S E L C I P I S D
_ Ⓞ _ _ _ _ _ _ _

T U D E M U L T I
_ _ Ⓞ _ _ _ _ _ _

PUZZLE: Which Fish?

Match each pair of fish by coloring each identically.

Queen Esther's Banquet

- ❏ **Theme:** God will help us solve problems. We need to pray and listen for God's answers.
- ❏ **Memory Verse:** "Trust in the LORD with all your heart and lean not on your own understanding" (Proverbs 3:5 NIV).
- ❏ **Nametags:** Crown pattern (see page 21)
- ❏ **Food:** A lavish potluck meal that includes turkey or chicken, boiled beans and peas, cheeses, braided bread decorated with raisins, kreplach (noodle pockets filled with meat—or ravioli can be used), hamantaschen (three-cornered cookie or cake filled with fruit), and grape juice. Note: Foods can be purchased in a Jewish grocery store.
- ❏ **Offering:** Ask each child to bring a pretty scarf and scarf clip. Donate these to a shelter that serves battered women.
- ❏ **Time:** 2 hours
- ❏ **Table Decorations:** Use lacy plastic table coverings. Choose a variety of colorful (pink, blue, purple, yellow) paper cups, plates, and napkins. You can use colorful patterns too.
- ❏ **Room Decorations:** Decorate the room to look like a king's palace. Make two large chairs look like thrones. Paint palace backdrops (look in books about palaces for ideas). Make columns, spray paint them gold, and sprinkle them with gold glitter before the paint dries. Have palm plants and other castle artifacts on hand. Designate areas where children can create art projects, play games, and eat.
- ❏ **Costume Idea:** Those portraying Queen Esther, King Xerxes, and Mordecai will need to dress in costume. Let children don costumes too, if desired.

Esther was the queen of Persia. Haman wanted to kill all the Jewish people, but Esther found a way to save her people. Invite the children to share in this banquet, which can be celebrated in connection with Purim, the Jewish festival that celebrates Esther's saving her people from Haman.

QUEEN ESTHER'S BANQUET
PROGRAM

Welcome: Welcome everyone and tell them they are going to learn about the time when the Persians had a banquet that lasted for 180 days.

 Activity: Queen Esther (Book of Esther). See page 43.

 Game: Lost in the Palace (see page 43)

 Art: Something for Mom (see page 43)

Song: "Queen Esther" (Sung to "Battle Hymn of the Republic")

> Queen Esther was a very, very, very brave queen.
> She helped her people, even those she'd never, ever seen.
> She was kind and good and holy, and was never, never mean.
> She really was a great, great queen.
> Hallelujah, let's praise Esther!
> Hallelujah, let's praise Esther!
> Hallelujah, let's praise Esther!
> For being such a brave and great queen!

 Art: Noise Makers (see page 44).

SOMETHING SPECIAL

Choose one of these books to share.

The Festival of Esther by Maida Silverman

Purim by Molly Cone

Grace: "Yeah, God!" (Encourage the kids to be enthusiastic.)

Leader:	God created great food for us to eat!
All:	Yeah, God!
Leader:	Name your favorite food!

Each child gets a turn to shout out their favorite food. After each food is shouted out, the rest of the group responds with "Yeah, God!"

Leader:	Thank you, God, for creating such great food for us to eat!
All:	Yeah, God!

Meal: Enjoy the banquet. Explain the significance of each of the foods being served. A gobbling turkey who struts around reminds us of the foolish king of Persia. Esther kept the dietary laws of her Jewish religion by eating peas and beans. Braided bread is enjoyed at all Jewish holidays. The kreplach are Haman's ears, and the hamantaschen reminds us of Haman's hat. While kids are eating, take instant photos of each one enjoying the feast. You need these to complete the bulletin board. Let the kids have fun posing for the photos.

 Bulletin Board: A Royal Feast (see page 44)

Closing: "We Love You, God" (Let a child lead it.)

> Thank you for loving us, God. Thank you for helping us work out problems. We love you God. Amen.

ACTIVITY
The Story of Esther

IDEAS

1. Ask Jewish friends or a rabbi to help you plan this celebration meal and suggest where to find the foods.

2. Consider celebrating this program with a nearby Jewish congregation.

Directions:

Have each actor help tell the story from his or her perspective. Let the actors choose their own words to share their experiences and feelings. Help the actors tell the story in such a way that it flows smoothly. Encourage them to use phrases such as "That's right!" "Well, after that happened," and so forth. The more the actors work to develop their own dialogue based on Scripture, the more familiar they will become with the story, and the better able they will be to "take on" the character they will portray.

After completing the story, they will remain in character for the duration of the program.

GAME: Lost in the Palace

Materials: 1 pendant per child, a pretty jewelry chest

Prior to the Program

1. Hide the pendants throughout the room or building. Consider hiding the pendants in a different room for each age group. This allows you to control the difficulty level.

2. Tape a few of the pendants to the underside of chairs, tables, or pews; hide them inside containers with lids; or slip them between things; and so forth. Make the game a challenge.

Directions

1. Open the jewelry chest and act astonished that the pendants are missing. Say, "This chest was filled with pendants. They must have been stolen by Haman. We have to find these pendants. I need you to help me."

2. Tell the kids which rooms each group will search. Say, "Each person is to find one, and only one, pendant. When you find one, quietly bring it back to me. Search silently so Haman doesn't see or hear you."

ART: Something for Mom

Explain that Purim is a time for giving of gifts. Today we are going to make a gift for our mothers. You can make additional necklaces and donate them to a shelter that works with abused women and children.

Materials: 1 thin 24- to 36-inch-long strand of sturdy leather per child, 1 pendant per child (look for a variety of inexpensive pendants and charms), a variety of colorful and shiny beads with holes large enough for the leather, masking tape

Directions

1. Give each child a leather string, a piece of masking tape, and one pendant. Have the children string the pendant on the leather.

HINTS ☺

1. Place each type of bead in a separate container. Cupcake tins work well for storing beads.

2. Encourage kids to be creative when designing their necklaces.

2. Let the children choose beads to string on the leather. Suggest that they place beads on each side of the pendant. Remind them to tape the end of the leather they are not holding to the table.

3. Once the necklace is complete, tie the ends together firmly. Remind the children to leave 2 to 3 inches of space at each end of the leather tie.

BULLETIN BOARD
A Royal Feast

Materials: shiny gold wrapping paper, shiny blue wrapping paper, stapler, letter stencils, color photos of food cut from magazines, camera loaded with instant film

The Bulletin Board

Prior to the Program

1. Cover the bulletin board with gold paper.
2. Trace the title "A Royal Feast" on the shiny blue paper. Cut the title out and attach it to the board.

Directions

1. Use the photos of each child that were taken during the banquet. Let each child put his or her photo on the bulletin board.
2. Add colored photos of food.

 ## ART: Noise Makers

Explain that kids have fun playing with noise makers at the Purim celebration.

Materials: dried beans, uncooked rice, small screws, and so forth; 1 small empty can with plastic lid (per child); glue; colored construction paper cut to fit around the outside of each can; glitter; sequins; markers; crayons; clear book tape

Directions

1. Tell each child to decorate one piece of construction paper with glitter, sequins, markers, and crayons. Glue paper to the outside of the can. Give the kids the rice, beans, screws, and so forth to put inside the can. They use one type of item or a combination of items.
2. Glue the lid to the top of the can. You might want to tape the lid to make sure it stays on.
3. Let the kids use their noise makers as part of the program.

PUZZLE
A Brave Queen

Follow the path to discover the message.

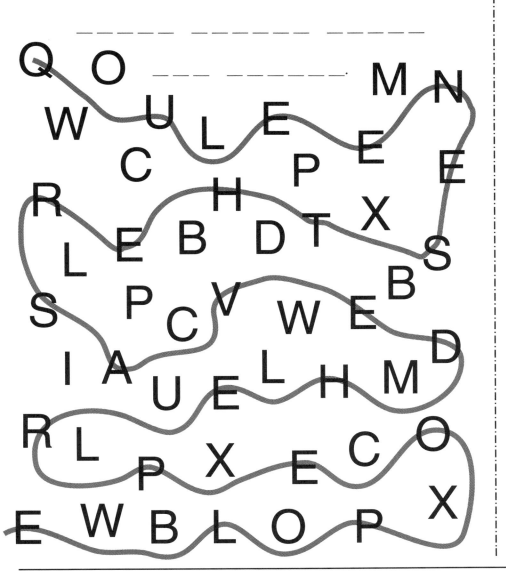

PUZZLE
Where's the Banquet Hall?

Find your way through the courtyard maze to get to the banquet hall.

FINISH!

START

Chapter 6 - Queen Esther's Banquet

CHAPTER 7

The Resurrection Cross Dinner

Hold this program during Lent. Keep the crosses the children make, and use them to decorate the sanctuary on Easter Sunday. Let the children take their crosses home at the conclusion of the Easter service as permanent Easter decorations. Invite children and parents to attend together.

☐ **Theme:** Jesus died on the cross to save us from our sins.

☐ **Memory Verse:** "The Lord has risen indeed . . ." (Luke 24:34).

☐ **Nametags:** Create nametags using the cross pattern on page 50. Use colored markers to print the child's name on the front and back. Punch a hole in the top of the nametag and string it with yarn. The nametag will slip over the child's head. Invite the children to use crayons to decorate the tags.

☐ **Food:** Have a potluck dinner with kid-friendly foods, such as chicken; macaroni and cheese; peanut butter and jelly sandwiches; chips; fruit; and juice. For dessert have white cupcakes with white frosting. Decorate them with flowers. Arrange the cupcakes in the form of a cross; place Easter grass and jelly beans around it.

☐ **Offering:** Ask each child to bring a new coloring book and a box of new crayons. Donate these to a local homeless shelter that works with families with children.

☐ **Time:** 1½ to 2 hours.

☐ **Table Decorations:** Use a variety of colorful spring tablecloths. Put a cross in the center of each table.

☐ **Room Decorations:** Display several samples of Resurrection crosses, including a large wooden cross (8 to 10 feet tall) to give the children an idea of what the Crucifixion cross might have looked like. On a window shade, paint a backdrop of Calvary (this can be a picture of the sky and hills). Place two large wooden crosses in front of the backdrop. Have the largest, heaviest cross lying on the floor. The children will "carry" this to Calvary later.

☐ **Room Setup:** Place the tables along the outside walls of the room. Use the center area for games and story sharing.

THE RESURRECTION CROSS DINNER

PROGRAM

Welcome: Welcome the children and explain that they are going to learn about the importance of the cross and will make Resurrection crosses that will be used to decorate the sanctuary on Easter.

Bible Story: The Crucifixion and Resurrection of Jesus (Matthew 27 and 28; Mark 15 and 16; Luke 23 and 24; John 18:28–21)

>
> ### SOMETHING SPECIAL
>
> Share the book *Easter* by Jan Pienkowski. This beautifully illustrated book can help you tell the children the story of the Crucifixion.

Tell the story of how Jesus was crucified, died on the cross, and rose from the dead. Jesus was placed between two robbers because people thought he was a criminal. They did not realize who Jesus was. On Easter, Mary and the other women went to the tomb to anoint Jesus' body with oil because that was Jewish custom.

 Game: Watch Calvary Bloom (see page 48)

Affirmation Ceremony: We Are All Children of Christ (see page 49)

 Activity: Carrying the Cross
Choose several children to take turns carrying the large cross alone. They will find it difficult, if not impossible, to lift. Let others help them carry it to Calvary. Once it is there, set it up, and tell the children that Jesus had to carry his own cross as he walked down the Via Dolorosa. Explain that Jesus was crucified on a cross like this, between two robbers, because many people did not believe that Jesus was the Savior.

> ### SOMETHING SPECIAL
>
> Read *The Tale of Three Trees* by Angela Elwell Hunt. Show the lovely illustrations. Locate a manger, a boat, and a cross as props for the story.

Art: The Resurrection Cross (see page 50)

Grace: "Thanks Be to God!" (Let a child lead this.)

Leader:	Thanks be to God for this time together.
All:	Thanks be to God!
Leader:	Thanks be to God for our food.
All:	Thanks be to God!

Dinner: Enjoy the potluck meal together. Show the children the cupcake cross.

Closing: "Thank You, God" (Let a child read this.)

> Thank you, God, for bringing us together today. Let us remember that Christ died on the cross to save us from our sins. Help us to share Christ's love with everyone we meet.

Song: "Share Christ's Blessings" (Sung to "Frere Jacques")

> Share Christ's blessings,
> Share Christ's blessings,
> With your friends,
> With your friends.

Let them know
Christ died for us.
Let them know Christ died for us.
Amen! Amen!

Sing each line and have the children repeat it after you. Then sing the song several times together. Next sing it as a round.

GAME
Watch Calvary Bloom

Materials: 2 long pieces of paper cut to fit bulletin board (cut one piece about 1 foot wider than the other); orange, red, yellow, and green powdered tempera paints; four paintbrushes; 3 to 9 flower-shaped sponges; black construction paper; gold shiny wrapping paper; lots of newspaper; 4 margarine tubs with covers; long table; masking tape; sponges

Prior to the Program

Do this several days prior to the program to allow paint to dry. This event helps create the bulletin board.

1. Mix one margarine tub of red, one of yellow, and one of orange paint. Mix them so that they are watery but retain their color. Paint a sunrise sky on the narrower piece of long paper. Blend the colors as you paint, so that they look like a sunrise sky. Let it dry.
2. Mix one margarine tub of green paint. Make it watery. Paint the wider length of paper green. Add yellow to give it a grassy appearance. Let it dry.
3. When the green strip is completely dry, use green paint to make flower stems and leaves on the hills. Let dry.
4. On the day of the program, mix one margarine tub each of red, yellow, and orange. Make them very thick.

5. Cover a long table with newspapers. Lay the green portion of the mural on top of the newspapers.
6. Put a masking tape line on the floor, so that it runs the length of the table (longer if necessary to accommodate the size of the group). Place the tape 3 feet away from the table.

Directions

1. Have the children sit along the line.
2. Select one to three children to paint at one time, depending on the size of your group.
3. Show the children how to dip the sponge into the paint and blot a flower stem without moving the sponge around on the mural. The imprint of the flower will show up. Let each child choose one color to paint. Children can blot paint flowers all over the hills.

Sing "Watch Calvary Bloom" as the mural is being painted. Keep those not painting seated on the line to avoid accidental bumps and spills.

Watch Calvary Bloom
(Sung to "Mary Had a Little Lamb")

Put the flowers on the hill, on the hill, on the hill;
Put the flowers on the hill, and watch Calvary bloom.

The children can sing this verse as the others paint. When the mural is completed sing the following:

Christ is our Savior, our Savior, our Savior.
Christ is our Savior, remember the risen Christ!

BULLETIN BOARD
Christ Is Risen!

Prepare the board early Easter Sunday morning before people arrive. Display it in a location where all members of your congregation can enjoy seeing it.

1. Cut three crosses from the black paper. One should be taller than the others.
2. Put the sky on the bulletin board.
3. Cut the green paper with the flowers so that it looks like three hills. Add it to the bulletin board.
4. On the tall cross use yellow chalk to print "Christ Is Risen!"
5. Cut the shiny, gold paper so that it looks like rays of the sun. Use it to frame the "Christ Is Risen" cross.
6. Add the crosses to the bulletin board, with one cross on each hill. The "Christ Is Risen" cross goes in the center.

Christ Is Risen!

The Bulletin Board

AFFIRMATION CEREMONY
We Are All Children of Christ

Materials: the children's nametags

Directions

1. Have the children stand in a circle. If parents are present, have parents stand behind their children. Ask the children to give their nametags to their parents. If parents are not present, collect the nametags and keep them until it is time to affirm each child individually.
2. Teach the children the responsive line "We are all children of Christ."
3. Tell the parents that when it is time for them to affirm their children to say, "_____ (name), I praise God for your _____ (list one good trait)."
4. Explain to the children that as they are affirmed individually, you want them to respond with "I am a child of Christ."

The leader takes a place in the circle until it is time to affirm each child individually.

Leader: You are all children of Christ.
Children: We are all children of Christ.
Leader: We come to affirm these children, Lord.
Children: We are all children of Christ.
Leader: God, you created these children. Each child is special.
Children: We are all children of Christ.

The leader moves to the center of the circle and goes to each child and says, "_____ (name), you are a child of Christ."

The parent puts the cross over child's head and says an affirming sentence about the child: "_____ (name), I praise God for your _____ (lists trait)." If parents are not present, the leader or another adult will affirm each child.

Child: I am a child of Christ.

When all the children have been affirmed say:

Leader: Thank you, God, for creating these children.
Children: We are all children of Christ.

ART
The Resurrection Cross

Materials: 1 large cross cut from white poster board per child (enlarge the cross pattern in a variety of sizes); 1 green garden or dowel rod (various lengths) per child (the shorter lengths go on smaller crosses, and longer on large crosses); white duct tape; 4 thin strands of colored ribbon (pink, blue, lavender, green, yellow, and orange) per child, cut into 12-inch lengths; glitter; 1 glue bottle with tip per child; black markers; yellow writing chalk; religious and Easter stickers; colored tissue paper; a list of Easter terms ("Christ," "Savior," "Lord," "rejoice," "love," "joy," "Jesus," "God," "praise," "Alleluia," and so forth); newspapers

Prior to the Program
1. Cover the tables with newspapers and set art supplies out.
2. Tape a dowel rod to the back of each cross.

Directions
1. Give each child a cross attached to a dowel rod, and a bottle of glue. Use a marker to print each child's first and last name on the back of their cross.

2. Give each child an Easter term, or let children choose one. Ask if they want their word to be written horizontally or vertically. An adult will use the glue bottles to print the term on the front of the cross. Make the lettering large.
3. Invite each child to sprinkle the glue with glitter. Let it set a few minutes, then shake off the excess glitter. Next, let the children use the ribbons, colored tissue paper, and stickers to decorate their crosses.
4. Lay crosses flat and allow to dry for twenty-four hours.
5. When decorating the sanctuary for Easter, add the crosses by inserting them into plants, taping them to the backs of pews, chairs, and so forth.
6. Let the congregation know that the children decorated the crosses for everyone to enjoy. After worship, the children can take their crosses home.

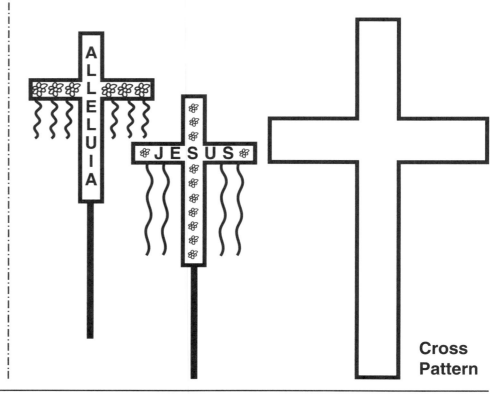

Cross Pattern

PUZZLE: *The Cross of Jesus*

Find the following words hidden inside the cross. Color each word yellow. The leftover letters spell an important message.

_____ _____ _____ _____ _____   _____ _____ _____ _____ _____ !

Which two words are listed twice? _____

Decorate your paper when you have finished the puzzle.

Resurrection
Jesus
You
My
Go
Cross
Bethlehem
Disciples
Angel
Lord
Awe
Miracle
Nazareth
Prayers
Me
Yes
Wow
Savior
Love
Hope
Baby
Lo

```
        J L O V E
        M E E H S
        Y E S O Y
        G O U P O
S L A L O R D E U B A B Y
W O W L B E T H L E H E M
I J E S U S S A V I O R Y
A N G E L U D C R O S S V
        E R I N P
        M R S A R
        I E C Z A
        R C I A Y
        A T P R E
        C I L E R
        L O E T S
        E N S H S
```

PUZZLE: *An Easter Cross*

Color: B=blue, G=green; R=red; O=orange; P=purple; K=pink, Y=yellow. Decorate the rest of your paper with Easter flowers.

CHAPTER 8

A Garden of Eden Fruit Festival

Consider using this program in connection with a series of lessons on the Creation story. Highlight the portions of the story that relate to God's creation of food. Talk about why God created food, especially fruits. Discuss Adam and Eve in the Garden of Eden. Consider holding the program in the spring when the fruit trees are blossoming. Also consider discussing how God created fruit trees that blossom and develop fruit. Encourage children to bring a friend.

❑ **Theme:** God created food to fulfill our need for nourishment.

❑ **Memory Verse:** " 'Let the earth put forth vegetation: plants yielding seed, and fruit trees of every kind on earth that bear fruit with the seed in it' " (Genesis 1:11).

❑ **Nametags:** Look for fruit-shaped nametags. Flannel-board books often include fruit-shaped patterns.

❑ **Food:** Fresh fruit salads that kids make in Activity (see page 54), apples, oranges, bananas, and so forth. Drink fresh fruit juices such as orange, cranberry, and grape.

❑ **Offering:** Ask each child to bring a large can of fruit, fruit juice, or a set of juice boxes. Donate these to a food pantry.

❑ **Time:** 1½ to 2 hours

❑ **Table Decorations:** Paper table coverings, plates, cups, and napkins with a fruit theme.

❑ **Room Decorations:** Locate large plants and pictures of fruits. Set up a large cornucopia with fruits spilling out. Paint a backdrop of the Garden of Eden, and place plants, flowers, and artificial grass in front of it. Designate areas for story sharing, games, art, and eating.

❑ **Costume Idea:** Wear tunics. Enlist volunteers to dress as Adam and Eve.

A GARDEN OF EDEN FRUIT FESTIVAL

PROGRAM

Welcome: Welcome everyone and explain that you are going to celebrate God's creation of fruits. Have Adam and Eve appear.

Bible Story: "God Creates Fruits" (Genesis 1:11-13)

Briefly retell the children the story of the Creation, then use flannelboard figures to tell how God created fruit trees, vines, and fruits. Be creative and add your own special touches to the presentation. Adam and Eve can help tell the story.

 Art: Fruit Paintings

Song: "Did You Ever Eat a _____ ?" (Sung to "Did You Ever See a Lassie?")

Did you ever eat a watermelon, a watermelon, a watermelon?
Did you ever eat a watermelon? It tastes so good!
It's juicy and squishy! It drips down your chin!
Did you ever eat a watermelon? It tastes so good!

Have the children think of verses to go with oranges, apples, bananas, and other fruits.

Activity: Outdoor Fun (see page 54)

Game: Yummy! (see page 54)

Activity: Fruit Salad (see page 54)

Bulletin Board: Fruity Fun (see page 55)

Grace: "Fabulous Fruits" (see page 55)

Meal: Share the fruit salad you created. Drink natural fruit juices for beverages.

Closing: Thank You, God, for Creating Fruits!

All: Thank you, God, for creating fruits!

Let the kids take turns yelling out the names of fruit. After each child yells out a fruit, respond with, "Thank you, God, for creating fruit."

All: We love fruit!

 ## ART: Fruit Paintings

Materials: 1 large piece of white heavy-duty construction paper per child; 1 large piece of colored construction paper per child (should be larger than the white sheet); tempera paints in a variety of colors and shades (mix them so that they are quite thick); disposable pie tins; rubber cement; newspapers; black marker; fruit rinds and peels (watermelon, orange, pineapple, banana); apples cut in half; paintbrushes

Prior to Program
Cover the tables with newspapers.

Directions

1. Let the children paint the rinds or peels to use to create prints on their white paper.
2. Use the marker to print child's name on paper.
3. When paper is dry, mount it on the colored paper.
4. Let children take these home.

ACTIVITY: Outdoor Fun

Materials: a variety of fruit seeds, an area for planting a fruit garden

Prior to the Program

1. Decide which fruits you want to plant (pumpkin, watermelon, and so forth).
2. Prepare the soil for planting.

Directions

1. Divide the children into groups of three or four and have each group plant one area of the garden.
2. Keep the area weeded and watered on a regular basis.
3. Watch the fruits grow. How much will you harvest in the fall?

GAME: Yummy!

Materials: pieces of fruits (bananas, apples, oranges, watermelon, cantaloupe, honeydew, and so forth), blindfolds

Directions

1. Teach kids this rhyme:

> It's yummy!
> It's nummy! It's in my tummy!

2. Blindfold several children at one time.
3. Place a piece of fruit in each child's mouth. Have each child say the rhyme and then tell what fruit they just ate. Do this until everyone has had a turn and all the fruits have been tasted. Use several fruits more than one time.

ACTIVITY: Fruit Salad

Materials: 1 large watermelon cut in half; honeydew; cantaloupe; pineapple; apples; seedless grapes; berries; melon ballers and other cutting implements; cutting boards; baby wipes

Prior to the Program

1. Cut the fruit out of the watermelon. Leave it in large chunks so that kids can cut it up later. Remove, wash, and dry the seeds. Put them aside. Scrape the inside of the watermelon well because it will become a fruit boat.
2. Cut honeydew and cantaloupes in half. Remove, wash, and dry the seeds. Put them aside.

Directions

1. Let the younger children use the melon baller to make honeydew and cantaloupe balls.
2. Older kids can cut up other fruits into bite-sized chunks. Supervise and teach children how to cut fruit safely.
3. Put the fruit pieces in the watermelon boat.
4. Refrigerate until it is time to eat.

Save the rinds for the Bulletin Board activity.

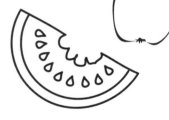

BULLETIN BOARD
Fruity Fun

Materials: white bulletin board paper; thick tempera paints in a variety of bright colors; watermelon, orange, cantaloupe, and honeydew rinds; banana peels; apples; pictures of watermelon, cantaloupe, oranges, honeydew, bananas, apples; newspapers; glue; paintbrushes; letter stencils; scissors; stapler

Prior to the Program
1. Cut the white paper to fit the bulletin board. Lay it on a flat table covered with newspapers.
2. Cut the apples in half. Peel the bananas. Cut melons and oranges away from rinds.
3. Trace the title "Fruity Fun" on colored construction paper. Cut it out and set it aside.
4. Mix temperas so they are thick.

Directions
1. Let the kids use the apples, banana peels, melon and orange rinds to make paint prints on the white paper, as they did for the fruit paintings.

The Bulletin Board

2. Intersperse their paintings with actual pictures of the fruit.
3. Add the title "Fruity Fun" to the painting. Let dry completely, then hang it on the bulletin board.

GRACE: *Fabulous Fruits*

Materials: plastic fruits (purchase from teacher stores, catalogs, or craft stores), large basket or cornucopia (often found in craft stores)

Prior to the Program
Place the plastic fruits in the basket or cornucopia.

Directions
1. Teach kids this rhyme:
   > Fabulous fruits, fabulous fruits!
   > I'm gonna eat some . . . fabulous fruits!
2. Blindfold each child or hold the basket overhead so that they cannot see inside.
3. Let the child reach in and pull out a fruit.
4. As a group, say the rhyme.
5. Let the child who chose the fruit say the verse alone, changing the final line to go along with the fruit he or she pulled out.
   > Fabulous fruits, fabulous fruits!
   > I'm going to eat an apple!
   > (Or whatever fruit the child draws.)
6. Play until everyone has had a turn.
7. End by saying:
   > Fabulous fruits! Fabulous fruits!
   > Let's thank God for fabulous fruits!

IDEA ✲

Use real fruits and let kids keep and eat what they choose from the basket.

PUZZLE
A Fruity Message

Fill in the missing letters to complete the names of the following fruits. The arrows tell you which direction each word goes. The letters in gray boxes spell out a special message.

PUZZLE
Fruit Matchup

Match the fruits by coloring each pair identically.

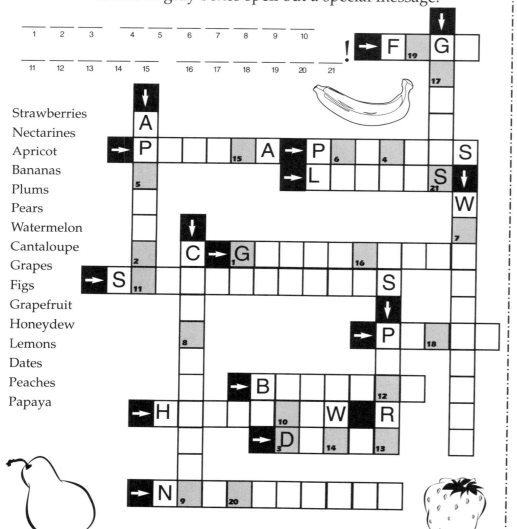

Strawberries
Nectarines
Apricot
Bananas
Plums
Pears
Watermelon
Cantaloupe
Grapes
Figs
Grapefruit
Honeydew
Lemons
Dates
Peaches
Papaya

56

BIBLE BANQUETS WITH KIDS

CHAPTER 9

Dinner with Mom

- ❏ **Theme:** Learning about biblical mothers. Consider using this program to begin a series of lessons on biblical mothers you choose to highlight.

- ❏ **Memory Verse:** "Do not reject your mother's teaching" (Proverbs 1:8*b*).

- ❏ **Nametags:** Choose any self-stick nametag.

- ❏ **Food:** A potluck meal featuring kid-friendly foods (Jell-O molds, fruit salads, celery and carrots, macaroni and cheese, fried chicken, cookies, brownies, fruit juices, milk, and so forth). Ask each family group to donate one item.

- ❏ **Offering:** Have each family group bring a package of disposable diapers to be donated to your food pantry. These can be given to mothers and children in need. Collect the gifts in large laundry baskets.

- ❏ **Table Decorations:** Cover the tables with white paper tablecloths. Put out crayons and markers, and let mothers and children decorate the tablecloths.

- ❏ **Room Setup:** Provide an area where moms and kids can sit on the floor together and listen to stories. Provide chairs for grandmothers, and a table for art projects and the meal. Have a camera and several rolls of color film. Take a photo of each mother and her children as they arrive. Include grandmothers in these photos too. Make one 5-by-7-inch print of each family. Make a separate print if a child's grandmother also attends. Make a list of the names of each family group's picture taken.

Invite children to bring their mothers to this special program for kids and moms. It is a perfect complement to Mother's Day. Children can bring their grandmothers too. Moms with adult children, and women without kids can also attend.

DINNER WITH MOM
PROGRAM

Welcome: Welcome the kids and their moms. Explain that they will learn about some interesting biblical moms and their kids.

Greeting: "Thanks for Moms and Their Kids"

Leader:	Thank you, God, for bringing all our mothers and their children together today.
Kids:	Thank you, God, for giving us mothers to love and care for us.
Mothers:	Praise God for giving us children to love and care for.
All:	Praise the Lord!

Bible Story: "Moses and His Mother" (Exodus 2:1-10). Make and present a flannel board of the story of Moses and his mother. Talk about the love Moses' mother had for him. Ask the mothers if they could do what Moses' mother did. Ask, How do you think she felt? Let the kids share their thoughts about the story.

Song: "Let's Praise the Lord" (Sung to "When the Saints Go Marching In")

Kids sing verse 1.

> Let's praise the Lord (*Clap, clap, clap, clap*)
> For our moms! (*Clap, clap, clap, clap*)
> Let's praise the Lord for all their love.
> Let's praise the Lord for what they do.
> Let's praise the Lord for our great moms!

Moms sing verse 2.

> Let's praise the Lord (*Clap, clap, clap, clap*)
> For our kids! (*Clap, clap, clap, clap*)
> Let's praise the Lord for all their love! Let's praise the Lord
> that we are mothers!
> Let's praise the Lord for our great kids!

Bulletin Board: Our Kids Are a Garden of Love (see page 59)

Story: "Free, Take One" (see page 61)

Project: Me and Mom (see page 60)

Bible Story: "Jesus and His Mother" (Matthew 1:1-23; Luke 2:1-20). Tell the story of how Mary became Jesus' mother. Recount all that she did for Jesus and how she sat near the cross at his crucifixion. (The Life Application Bible has a biography about Mary that may be helpful.)

Affirmation Ceremony: Praise God for Moms and Kids. The ceremony is found on pages 60-61.

Game: Buckets of Love (see page 61)

Grace: "Let's Give Our Thanks" (Sung to "The Bear Went Over the Mountain")

> Let's give our thanks, let's give our thanks,
> Let's give our thanks for all of this food.

SOMETHING SPECIAL

Share one of these stories.

Mama, Do You Love Me?
by Barbara Joose

Mother, Mother, I Want Another
by Maria Polushkin

I Love My Mommy Because
by Laurel Gaylad Porter

Mary of Nazareth
by Cecil Bodker

Mary, the Mother of Jesus
by Tomie dePaola

For all of this food, for all of this food.
Let's give our thanks for all of this food.

Meal: Enjoy a potluck dinner together.

Closing: Let a child lead this:

Thank you, God, for giving us mothers to love and care for us. Help us to show respect and love to our mothers. Amen.

BULLETIN BOARD
Our Kids Are a Garden of Love

Materials: instant camera and several rolls of instant film; crayons; blue construction paper; scissors; multicolored construction paper; markers; green construction paper; glue; purple, pink, red, orange, and yellow construction paper; white cotton; one flower cutout per family group (see bottom right); letter stencils; stapler

Prior to the Program
1. Cover the bulletin board with blue paper for the sky and green paper for the hills.
2. Trace the title "Our Kids Are a Garden of Love" on multicolored construction paper. Cut out the letters and staple them to the sky. Add a yellow sun and cotton clouds.

Directions
1. Have mothers and children sit together at the tables to work on this project.
2. Give each child a flower to color. As they work, take a candid photo of each child.

3. Have each child glue their photo to the center of the flower.
4. Ask moms to write on the petals things they like about their kids.
5. Staple the flowers to the bulletin board to make a garden.

The Bulletin Board

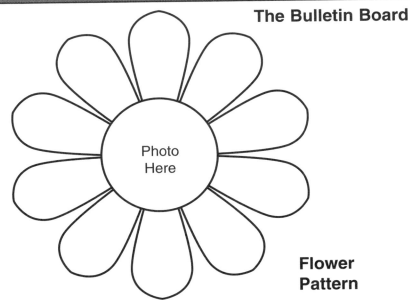

Photo Here

Flower Pattern

PROJECT: *Me and Mom*

Materials: one 8-by-10-inch cardboard frame with a 5-by-7-inch cutout (cut your own or purchase one at a craft store) in a variety of colors; one family photo (5 by 7 inches or larger); several different shaped sponges for each color; powdered tempera paints (blue, red, green, orange, yellow, purple); 1 paintbrush per color; 8-by-10-inch envelope; 6 disposable large pie tins; card stock paper (8 by 10 inches); newspapers; rubber cement

Prior to the Program
Mix paints so that they are quite thick. Put one color into each pie tin.

Directions
1. Give each family group a picture frame. If grandmothers are present, supply an additional frame for each grandmother.
2. Let each family group use the sponges and paints to decorate their frames. Use one sponge to each color. If grandmothers are present, let the children and grandmothers also decorate a frame.
3. Label each family's frame with their name. Let dry overnight.
4. Use rubber cement to mount each photo on a piece of 8-by-10-inch card stock paper. Mount it in the center, so that it will show through the 5-by-7-inch opening in the cardboard frame.
5. Use rubber cement to attach the photo to the frame. Send them to each family.

AFFIRMATION CEREMONY
Praise God for Moms and Kids

Materials: 1 Christmas candlelight candle per family group, cassette player, an audio cassette tape of soothing instrumental music

Directions
1. Have everyone stand in a large circle. The adults can stand behind the children. The mother will hold the family candle.
2. The leader should stand in the center of the circle with a lit candle.
3. Explain that the word "affirm" means to compliment someone.
4. Go around the circle and have each mother say something affirming about her children. ("I thank God for your willingness to help your sister." "Thank you for helping with your chores.") After each child is affirmed, the mothers will respond with "Thanks be to God for our children."
5. Then let each child say something affirming about their mother. ("Thanks for making me lunch every day." "Thanks for driving the carpool.") After each mother is affirmed, children will respond with "Praise God for our mothers."

Leader: Praise God for these mothers and children.
Mothers: Praise God for creating our children. They are a blessing from God.
Children: Praise God for our mothers. They are a gift from God.

Go around the circle. Stop by the first family group and light the candle held by the mother. Let the mother use one sentence to affirm each child.

Mothers: Thanks be to God for our children!

Let each child in that family group say a one-sentence affirmation about their mother.

Children: Praise God for our mothers!

Leader: God, we thank you for giving each of these women the gift of motherhood. Give them the strength to raise their children to be respectful citizens. Help them teach their children about your love. Let each of the children show their love for their mothers by treating them with kindness and respect.

All:　　Praise God from whom all blessings flow.

The mothers blow out the candles.

GAME: *Buckets of Love*

Materials: 4 large buckets; bean bags; 1 prize per person (samples of lotion, shampoo, and so forth for the moms; small toys for kids); blue and green tissue paper; ribbon; masking tape

HINT ⊚

Adapt throwing distance according to the age and ability of the children.

Prior to the Program

1. Label each bucket with one letter of the word "love."
2. Wrap the moms' prizes in the green tissue paper, and kids' prizes in the blue tissue paper. Tie with ribbon and put prizes in the buckets.
3. Put a masking-tape line on the floor.

Directions

1. Set the buckets in a row so that they spell out "love."
2. One at a time, each person can stand behind the line and try to throw a bean bag into one of the buckets.
3. When a throw is successful, the person gets to reach inside and choose a prize.

STORY: *Free, Take One*

Make pictures and a coupon book to show the kids while sharing this story with moms and kids.

"What am I going to do?" thought Kevin as he wandered through the store looking for just the right gift for Mother's Day. All of the gifts he had seen cost more money than he had. "If I hadn't bought that computer game last week, I would have enough money. How's Mom going to feel tomorrow when I don't give her a Mother's Day present?" Kevin said to himself.

All week at school his friends had been talking about what they were buying their mothers.

"I've bought my mom a necklace," said Elisa.

"I'm going to give my mom a scarf," said Ashley.

"You should smell the perfume I got for my mom," said Joseph.

Kevin was about to leave the store when he spotted a sign—"Free, Take One."

So Kevin took one and looked at it. It was a booklet of coupons. The coupons were for all sorts of things. You could buy something and receive something else for free. There were two-for-the-price-of-one coupons. Some coupons gave the buyer money off the full price of something.

Suddenly, Kevin had an idea. He ran home as fast as he could. He went right to his room. He put a sign on the door that said, "I'm Very Busy. Please Do Not Disturb. Thank You."

Kevin worked hard all afternoon. When he was finished, he turned off the computer and put his crayons and paints away. He went outside to play before dinner.

Early the next morning, Kevin got up and went to work. He had to work fast and quietly. He taped papers all over the house. He wrapped the final present in pretty paper and hid it in the piano bench.

Soon Kevin's parents got up. His mom opened the bedroom door and found a greeting card taped to the outside of the door. The card said, "Free, Take One." Kevin's mom opened the card; inside there was a picture of her that Kevin had drawn. Under the picture were the words "You Are The Best Mom In The Whole Entire World!" She found a sign on the mirror in the hall. The sign said, "Thanks For Helping Me With My Math." In the kitchen there was a picture of her cooking. It said, "You Are The Bestest Cook!" His mom went to the front door to get the morning paper. A sign on the door said, "Thanks For Driving Me And My Friends Places." In the living room she found the biggest sign of all.

The sun is yellow,
The sky is blue.
There's no mom in the world
Who's greater than you!

If you give the bench a lift,
Inside you will find a gift.
Thanks for being my mom!

HAPPY MOTHER'S DAY!
Love, Kevin

Kevin's mom opened the piano bench and took out the gift. She unwrapped it. It was a book of coupons. She looked through the book. It was filled with marvelous offers—two for the price of one! "I'll give you two good-bye kisses every day for a week," one coupon read. Another coupon said, "SPECIAL OFFER. I'll help you weed the garden, even though I hate it." Another coupon said, "FREE OFFER: I'll do three extra chores without being paid."

The last coupon said, "I'll Never Stop Loving You No Matter What!"

Kevin came into the living room. "You've given me the best Mother's Day present in the whole wide world!" said his mom. "It took lots of work and thinking to make all of these pictures and coupons. Thank you, Kevin, for being such a great son!"

PUZZLE

What Do Moms Do All Day?

Can you find the following words in the puzzle? Circle the leftover letters and write them in the spaces below to spell out a special message.

___ ___ ___ ___   ___ ___ ___

___ ___ ___ ___ ___   ___ ___ ___ !

VOLUNTEER	READ TO ME	COOK	IRON
WASH CLOTHES	ENCOURAGE	WORK	CARE
DRIVE CARPOOLS	PRAISE	HELP	SEW
PLAY GAMES	HUG ME	TEACH	CLEAN

MCLEANOVOLUNTEERMHUGMESWORKLWASHCLOTHESOENCOURAGEVHELPECOOKTREADTOMEHPLAYGAMESEPRAISEICARERTEACHKIRONIDRIVECARPOOLSDSEWS

Use a sheet of paper to make a Mother's Day card. Draw a picture and tell why you like having her as your mom. Sign your name. You can fold your paper any way you choose.

CHAPTER 10

A Pentecost Picnic

☐ **Theme:** Celebrating the birth of Christianity, and sharing the Good News with all we meet

☐ **Memory Verse:** "For the promise is for you, for your children, and for all who are far away, everyone whom the Lord our God calls to him" (Acts 2:39).

☐ **Nametags:** Use the dove-shaped nametag on page 67.

☐ **Food:** Since dairy foods are often eaten out of respect for the commandment "Do not kill," provide fruit-flavored yogurt; fruit; vegetables; breads; cheeses; pita sandwiches; and grape juice. Have a cake decorated with red flames or cut in the shape of a cross or dove to celebrate the birthday of the church. Insert one red candle.

☐ **Offering:** Ask each family or individual to bring nonperishable foods, which will be donated to a food pantry.

☐ **Time:** 2 hours

☐ **Table Decorations:** White tablecloths. Cut flames from red, orange, and yellow construction paper and glue them to the table coverings.

☐ **Room Decorations:** Decorate the area to resemble the Upper Room. Provide an area for kids to create art projects, play games, and eat.

Passover is celebrated by Jewish people in March or April. Fifty days later they celebrate the Feast of Weeks, which occurs at the end of the grain harvest (Deuteronomy 16:9-16). This celebration is also called Pentecost. After Jesus rose from the dead, he spent the next weeks with his disciples. Forty days later he ascended into heaven, and ten days later everyone gathered to celebrate the Feast of Weeks (Pentecost). That year, the Holy Spirit descended upon the people.

Pentecost, which means "fifty," is the birthday of the Christian church. It occurs fifty days after Passover and the Resurrection of Jesus. Jewish people celebrate Pentecost, or the Feast of Weeks, so they can thank God for the gift of harvested grain crops. The Feast of Weeks also commemorates the giving of the Ten Commandments. If desired, include a brief dramatization of the Ten Commandments during the program. Let this be an intergenerational program for the entire congregation.

A PENTECOST PICNIC
PROGRAM

Welcome: Welcome everyone. Explain that you are going to celebrate a festival called the Feast of Weeks.

Many years ago, before Jesus was born, Jewish people would gather fifty days after Passover to celebrate the end of the harvest season. They gave thanks to God for the crops they had grown. This celebration was also called Pentecost, which means "fifty." However, at the Pentecost celebration following Jesus' death, something different happened. That's what we're going to learn about.

Opening: "Thanks Be to God!" (Let a child lead this.)

    Leader: God loves us!
    All: Thanks be to God!

Bible Story: "The Holy Spirit Comes at Pentecost" (Acts 2)

Song: "I Give My Heart to You" (Sung to "Michael, Row the Boat Ashore")

    I give my heart to God; Alleluia!
    I give my heart to you; Alleluia!
    I give my heart to Christ; Alleluia!
    I give my heart to you; Alleluia!
    I will praise God and Christ; Alleluia!
    I will praise the Holy Spirit; Alleluia!

Art: Flames of Love (see page 65)

Game: Find the Disciples (see page 65)

Bulletin Board: The Gift of the Holy Spirit (see page 67)

Bible Story: "The Ten Commandments" (see page 67)

Grace: "God's Love Came Down" (Sung to "When the Saints Go Marching In")

    God's love came down,
    And filled our hearts!
    God's love filled our hearts with love.
    Let us praise God's holy name,
    And celebrate this feast with thanks!

    Thanks be to God,
    For giving food!
    God nourishes our hearts and souls.
    Let us praise God's holy name,
    And celebrate this feast with thanks!

Meal: Have an outdoor picnic, if the weather permits. Or sit on the floor in groups and enjoy the feast. Light the candle on the cake and say a prayer, thanking Jesus for his love.

Closing: "Thanks Be to God!" (Let a child lead this.)

    All: Thanks be to God!
               Thanks be to God!
               Thanks be to God! Amen!

BIBLE STORY: The Holy Spirit Comes at Pentecost

Materials: fiberfill clouds suspended with fishline from the ceiling; large fans; audiocassette sound effects of wind blowing;

audiocassette player; red cloth cut in the shape of flames (1 per person); two scrolls with the lines printed on them. (Use two paper towel cardboard tubes. Print Acts 2:14-36 on long sheets of white paper. Attach the paper to the cardboard tubes with tape to make a scroll for each actor.)

Adults or teens can portray the disciples and others in this story. Enlist people who speak a variety of languages—Spanish, French, Italian, and so forth. The more languages you have, the better. (Each person can recite the Lord's Prayer in a different language.) An adult will be needed to portray Peter, one to narrate, and one to portray the Holy Spirit (dressed in white flowing material).

Directions

Practice before presenting the story to your audience.

1. The narrator begins by explaining that the people had gathered to celebrate the Feast of Weeks: "Well, this year when they gathered to celebrate this festival, something awesome happened. Let us tell you about it."
2. The narrator tells the story, beginning with Acts 2:1. Turn on the fans and sound effects tape; and let the tape play as the Holy Spirit places the tongues of fire upon each person in the story.
3. The people begin "speaking in tongues" (recite the Lord's Prayer in the different languages).
4. Peter then delivers his speech (Acts 2:14-36).
5. The narrator completes the story, and explains that this is the birthday of the Christian church.
6. Afterward, talk to the children about all that Christianity offers us.

 ART: *Flames of Love*

Materials: 1 dove per person cut from white card stock (see pattern on page 67); red powdered tempera paint; one 9-by-11-inch sheet of white card stock per person; book tape; 1 small paint sponge per child; disposable pie tins, newspapers

Prior to the Program

1. Mix the tempera so that it is thick. Place a small amount in each pie tin.
2. Tape the doves to the center of the card stock paper. Place pieces of tape on the back of each dove.

Directions

1. Give each child a piece of paper with a dove taped to it.
2. Invite the children to sponge paint around the dove, making sure to touch the edges of the dove all the way around. Show them how to dab the sponge on a piece of newspaper to soak up the excess paint.
3. Have them carefully lift the dove from the paper, leaving a dove print.

IDEAS ✷

If you have unbaptized children or adults in attendance, this would be a good time for your pastor to conduct a baptism.

 **GAME:** *Find the Disciples*

Materials: 1 prize per child

Ask 11 adults to portray the disciples, and one adult to accompany each group of four kids.

Directions

1. Design an age-appropriate treasure hunt for each group of kids. The kids will follow clues to find the disciples. Ask an adult to accompany each group during the hunt. Vary the difficulty of locations. Some can be easy to find, while others are harder to find.
2. Have each disciple hide.
3. As each group finds all the disciples, each child will be given a prize.
4. Tell each group to keep "disciples locations" a secret from the other teams.

SAMPLE TREASURE HUNT FOR PRE-SCHOOL AND KINDERGARTEN

1. Do you know where Jesus died? (On the cross.) Where can we go to find a cross? (In the sanctuary.) *Let the kids lead you to the sanctuary where they can look for a disciple near the cross on the altar. The disciple will give them Clue 2.*

HINT

The adults working with the younger kids may have to provide additional clues and help them actually look. Older kids can handle more challenging clues, and can be allowed to hunt on their own with the accompanying adult just watching.

2. Where do babies go during church? (The nursery.) *Let the kids lead you to the nursery. The disciple there will give them Clue 3.*
3. Where does the choir sit in church? (In the choir loft.) *Have a disciple hiding on the floor of the choir loft. He will give the next Clue 4.*
4. Where do you go to learn about Jesus? (Sunday school.) *Let them show you their Sunday school room. The disciple will be there with Clue 5.*
5. Where do they make food for the meals we have at church? (In the kitchen.) *Let the kids lead you to the kitchen where a disciple will give them Clue 6.*
6. Where does Pastor _____ (name) do his/her work? (In his/her office.) *Go to the pastor's office where the disciple will give them Clue 7.*
7. Where does the church secretary work? (In the church office.) *Let them show you where the secretary works. The disciple there will give them Clue 8.*
8. Where do people come inside the church on Sunday morning? (The narthex, entry, lobby.) *Go to the narthex by the entrance. The disciple there will give them Clue 9.*
9. Where can we go to find books to read? (The church library.) *Go to the library where a disciple will give you Clue 10.*
10. Where do the first-graders meet? (In a classroom.) *Go to the first-grade classroom where a disciple will give you Clue 11.*
11. Where did we start this treasure hunt? (In the fellowship hall.) *Have the kids find fellowship hall. The disciple there will give each of them a prize.*

IDEAS

1. Older kids can be given word puzzles to solve that will provide hints as to where to find clues.
2. Include two or three clues where older kids have to use their Bibles to look up the answers.
3. Have some of the clues inside plastic, colored eggs. Younger kids can open the eggs to get the clue. For older children, print the name of a hymn on separate squares of paper. Print one word per square or one letter per square. Hide the squares inside an egg. Have one of the disciples provide the egg with the hint inside. When the kids open the egg, they must figure out what the hymn is. Then they must look it up in the index of the hymnal that happens to be sitting nearby. Attached to the correct page is a sticky paper with the next clue written on it. Be sure to mark each egg, so you know which age group it is for.
4. Print a clue on a strip of paper and put it inside a balloon. Provide one blown-up balloon with a clue per group of kids. They must pop the balloons to get the clue.
5. Use rhymes, Bible verses, and so forth as clues. The clue can be one of the words in a Bible verse or rhyme.
6. If your church has a balcony, use it as a hiding place.

BIBLE BANQUETS WITH KIDS

BULLETIN BOARD
The Gift of the Holy Spirit

Materials: 1 large bulletin board; bright blue paper to cover the bulletin board; heavy white construction paper; red, yellow, and orange finger paints; scissors; stapler; large white dove cut from white card stock (enlarge pattern below); white glitter; glue; movable eye; newspapers; letter stencils

The Bulletin Board

Prior to the Program
1. Glue white glitter and the movable eye to the dove.
2. Cut white paper to look like tongues of fire.

Directions
1. Cover the table with newspapers. Spread the tongues of fire on top.
2. Let the kids take turns using their fingers to paint the flames. Dab each child's fingers with a combination of red, orange, and yellow paints. Different fingers will be different colors.
3. Tell the kids to paint the white paper. Show them how to make long sweeping motions with their fingers. The white flames should be completely covered with paints.

Dove & Flames Pattern

4. When the flames dry completely, staple them to the bottom of the board so that it looks like they are reaching upward. Add the dove, which should appear to be flying above the flames.
5. Add the title, using the stencil letters.

BIBLE STORY
The Ten Commandments

Materials: mountain scene painted on a white window shade; two tablets (made from plaster of paris) with the Ten Commandments written on them (See Exodus 20:1-17.)

Make the scenery look as if Moses will be standing in the mountains. Place a tree stump next to the scene. Position the shade and stump at the far end of the room. This dramatization will need one adult to portray Moses, and one (behind the scenery) to play God (choose someone in the church that the children do not readily know).

Directions
1. Have Moses wander into the room, introduce himself, and ask for directions to Mount Sinai. Tell him how to get there. Continue with what you were doing.
2. Once he arrives and sits on the mountain, God will begin to speak. Everyone will then direct their attention to the mountain where Moses is sitting. God can then deliver the Ten Commandments.
3. Have Moses take the tablets and leave.
4. Ask the children if they can tell you what just happened.
5. Remind kids that Pentecost celebrates God's giving Moses the Ten Commandments.

IMPORTANT

God should not be seen by anyone. You want the children to think that God is actually speaking. Have the actor hide behind the backdrop.

PUZZLE
What Is God Trying to Tell Us?

Unscramble the words inside each of the flames.
The circled letters spell out a message.

What's the message? _____

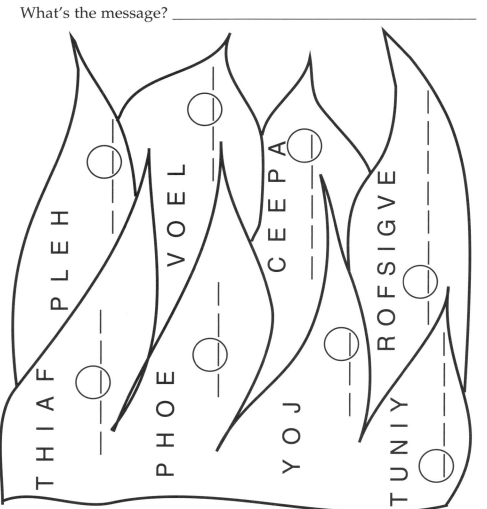

THIAF PLEH

PHOE VOEL

CEEPA YOJ

ROFSIGVE TUNIY

PUZZLE
What Do You See in the Flames?

Connect the dots to see what is in the
flames. Then color your picture.

44
• 43
• 41
42 • • 40
45 • 39 • 38
37 •
1 48 47
2   • 36
3   46
6   5   34   33
35   31 • • 32
7   29 • • 30
8   27
9   16   19   21   25   28
12   13   20   26
10 11 14 15 17 18   22 24
23

CHAPTER 11

A Cookout with Dad

- ❏ **Theme:** Learning about biblical fathers. In addition, this lesson can be used to begin a series on fathers in the Bible.

- ❏ **Memory Verse:** "Hear, my child, your father's instruction" (Proverbs 1:8*a*).

- ❏ **Nametags:** Use self-stick nametags.

- ❏ **Food:** Hamburgers, hot dogs, buns, chicken, ribs, and so forth. Ask each family group to bring the food of their choice. Provide lemonade, condiments, chips, cookies, paper plates, and cups.

- ❏ **Offering:** Ask each family group to bring a newly purchased tool (hammer, screwdriver, wrench, and so forth). Put the tools in a large toolbox and donate them to a local agency that helps families in need.

- ❏ **Time**: 2 hours

- ❏ **Table Decorations:** If the weather permits, eat outdoors. Have a table covered with a plastic tablecloth. Put the food on this table, and eat sitting at tables or on the ground.

- ❏ **Room Setup:** Provide tables for art activity and project, and designate an area where kids and dads can sit and listen to stories.

- ❏ **Camera and Film:** Have a camera and several rolls of film on hand.

Invite kids to bring their dads to a cookout, which could be held in connection with Father's Day in June. Include granddads as well, and ask adult children and their dads to serve as chefs, storytellers, and game leaders.

Enlist several people to bring outdoor grills. Have the chefs cook the foods during the program, so that everything is ready when it is time to eat. If necessary, ask people to pay a small fee to cover the cost of the photos used in the program.

A COOKOUT WITH DAD
PROGRAM

Welcome: Tell everyone that we are going to have fun learning about biblical dads and their kids.

Greeting: "Let's Thank God for Dads and Kids" (This is a rap. Alternate clapping and snapping fingers on each syllable.)

Leader:	Let's thank God for bringing us together!
Kids:	Thank you, God, for our dads!
Fathers:	Thank you, God, for our kids!
All:	Praise God, praise God, praise God, praise God! (*Speak, clap/snap fast.*) Praaaaaaaaaaaise GOD! (*Shout without clapping/snapping.*)

SOMETHING SPECIAL ❧

Use one of these books to help you tell the story.

Children's Bible Stories from Genesis to Daniel by Miriam Chaikin

Tomie dePaola's Book of Bible Stories by Tomie dePaola

Stories from the Bible: Old Testament Stories Retold by Martin Waddell

---

Bible Story: Tell about Abraham and his large family; consider using story cards (Genesis 12:1–25:18). Choose which Scripture portions you want to cover.

Song: "Let's Praise the Lord" (Sung to "When the Saints Go Marching In")

Kids sing verse 1.

> Let's praise the Lord (*Clap, clap, clap, clap*)
> For our dads! (*Clap, clap, clap, clap*)
> Let's praise the Lord for all their love.
> Let's praise the Lord for all they do.
> Let's praise the Lord for our great dads! (*Clap, clap, clap, clap*)

Dads sing verse 2.

> Let's praise the Lord (*Clap, clap, clap, clap*)
> For our kids! (*Clap, clap, clap, clap*)
> Let's praise the Lord for all their love.
> Let's praise the Lord that we are fathers!
> Let's praise the Lord for our great kids! (*Clap, clap, clap, clap*)

 Art: Dads and Their Kids (see page 71)

Story: "Whatever You Wish" (see page 73)

Project: Me and Dad (see page 71)

Bible Story: "Joseph and Jesus" (Matthew 1:18-24, 2:13-23; Luke 2:1-52). Tell how Joseph came to be Jesus' earthly father. Explain that Joseph taught Jesus to be a carpenter. (The Life Application Bible has a biography of Joseph.)

Affirmation Ceremony: Praise the Lord for Dads and Kids (see page 72)

BIBLE BANQUETS WITH KIDS

Game: Where Are the Prizes? (see page 72)

Grace: "Let's Give Thanks" (Sung to "The Bear Went Over the Mountain")

Let's give our thanks, let's give our thanks,
Let's give our thanks for all of this food.
For all of this food, for all of this food.
Let's give our thanks, let's give our thanks,
Let's give our thanks for all of this food!

Meal: Enjoy the cookout together.

Closing: "Thanks for Dad" (Let a child lead this.)

God, thank you for giving us dads to love and care for us. Please help us show we love and respect them. Amen.

SOMETHING SPECIAL 🎗

Share one of these stories.

My Dad Is Magnificent by Kristy Parker

Daddy Makes the Best Spaghetti by Anna Grossnickle Hines

Daddy, Could I Have an Elephant? by Jake Wolf

ART
Dads and Their Kids

Materials: 1 large bulletin board covered with brightly colored paper; instant camera and film; 1 instant photo of each dad and his kids (include granddads who attend); stapler; markers; white paper strips (6 by 2 inches)

Directions

1. Take a photo of each dad with his kids, including granddads who are in attendance. Staple the photos to the bulletin board, so that they spell out "Dad."
2. Have each father, grandfather, and child autograph a strip of paper. Staple these next to the appropriate photos on the bulletin board.
3. Make a sign that says "Dads and Their Kids" to hang on the wall above the bulletin board.

PROJECT: Me and Dad

Materials: instant camera and film, 1 wooden plaque per family group (Stain plain wooden plaques or purchase plaques that look like sections of a tree. Provide a separate plaque for the grandfathers.); decoupage solution; photo of each family (If granddads attend, take one extra family photo for each of them.); 1 paintbrush per family group; 1 picture hanger for each plaque; scissors

Prior to the Program

Attach the picture hangers to the back of each plaque.

Directions

1. Give each family group one plaque and paintbrush. Brush decoupage solution on the plaque. Place the picture in the center of the plaque and press firmly so that it sticks. Trim photos, if necessary, to fit the plaques. Allow each granddad to make a separate plaque.
2. Let dry, and take home.

AFFIRMATION CEREMONY
Praise the Lord for Dads and Kids

Materials: a large flashlight; 1 wooden cross on a piece of leather (per child); audiocassette player; a tape of jazzy, kids' music

Directions

1. Have the kids form a circle, with their dads standing behind them.
2. Give each dad a cross to hold.
3. Play the music softly.

> **Leader:** Praise God for creating fathers.
> **Fathers:** Thanks be to God for making us fathers!
> **Kids:** Thanks be to God for our great dads!

The leader, standing in the center, goes around the circle and shines the flashlight on each child's face as each dad says something affirming about

his child. ("Elizabeth, I praise God for your musical talent.") In return, each child can say something affirming about their dad. ("Dad, thanks for playing ball with me.") Each dad will then put the cross over his child's head. Let granddads who are present take part in this by affirming their sons and/or grandchildren. After everyone has had a chance to speak, continue with the following:

> **Leader:** Praise God for these wonderful fathers who love their children.
> **Fathers:** Praise the Lord!
> **Kids:** Praaaaaaaise God!

GAME
Where Are the Prizes?

Materials: 1 ball or other toy that dads and kids can use together; 1 bucket per group; audiocassette of kids' songs and audiocassette player; envelopes with clue cards inside

Prior to the Program

1. Make one clue card for each prize that you hide. The card will give hints about where to find the prize. (Examples: The choir sings from here on Sunday morning. [The choir loft.] We see one of these when the sun shines during a rainstorm. [Under the rainbow stained-glass window.] Make these appropriate to your church.)
2. Hide prizes outdoors and/or in the church building. Make it challenging.
3. Put clue cards inside the envelopes. Seal envelopes and put them in the bucket. Depending on the size of the group, you may need several buckets filled with clue cards. Make sure

there is one envelope per family group inside each bucket. Have a few extras on hand.

Directions

1. Have dads and kids sit side by side on the floor in a large circle.
2. Hand the bucket to one of the dads. Tell him to hang on to it until the music starts. Then pass it to the right.
3. Play the music. Stop the music. The person holding the bucket when the music stops takes out an envelope. That family group leaves the circle, reads the card, and goes to find the prize. Afterward, they can return to the room. Play until every group has found a prize.

STORY
Whatever You Wish

Prior to the Program

Make a treasure map like the one mentioned in the story. Also make each of the puzzles and envelopes. To make the painting puzzle, use white crayon to write the words "Go Climb a Tree" on white paper. Press very heavily, going over each letter many times. Have water and blue watercolor paint.

Use the props as you come to each of them in the story. The story tells you how, but it is a good idea to practice before sharing it with your guests.

The trouble began when Kevin and his friends decided to play baseball in the yard. Kevin was not very good at baseball, but that day he hit the ball farther than he had ever hit it. It went right through the window of his next-door neighbor's garage. CRASH! Mr. Morris came out to see what had broken his window. Kevin went over to the fence and apologized to him. Kevin's father went out to see what was going on. When he found out what had happened, he told Kevin to get the money out of his bank and give it to Mr. Morris for a new window.

"But, Dad, that's my money! I saved it from my allowance and from walking all those dogs!" exclaimed Kevin.

"Kevin, I know you worked hard to save that money, but you broke Mr. Morris's window. Now you have to pay to replace it," said Kevin's father.

"But it was an accident. I didn't do it on purpose. I said I was sorry," said Kevin.

"I know that, Kevin. Even though it was an accident, you still have to pay for a new window. Go get your money," said his father.

Kevin got the money and gave it to Mr. Morris.

After his friends went home, Kevin climbed into his tree house to think about what had happened. "What am I going to do about Father's Day?" he wondered. "Now, I don't have any money, so I can't buy that book for Dad."

Kevin was still sitting in the tree house when his parents came to the patio to relax. They didn't know Kevin was in the tree house. One of Kevin's books was on the table.

Kevin's father picked it up. "The Three Wishes," he read. "I read this to Kevin the other day. He enjoyed it."

"You know Kevin and his imagination," said his mother. "I wonder what he'd wish for."

"I can tell you what I'd wish for," said Kevin's dad.

"What?" asked Kevin's mother.

"First, I'd wish for a long walk in the woods. My second wish would be to go on a weekend camping trip. I'd go to a quiet place and catch fish to eat, look at the stars and enjoy nature. My third wish would be to spend a day doing puzzles. I never have time for them."

Kevin had an idea. He waited until his parents went into the house. Then he climbed down out of the tree house and went to his room. His parents were busy preparing dinner, so he knew he had time to work.

Kevin worked with his computer and art supplies for a long time. When he was finished, he put everything away and went down to dinner.

The next Sunday was Father's Day. Kevin woke up early and went to work. He hid three boxes in the yard. Next, he hid envelopes all over the yard. He put one envelope by his father's place at the breakfast table.

When Kevin's dad found the envelope, which had a message on it printed backward, he took it over to the mirror and held it up. The message said, "Open Carefully." When he opened it, he was surprised to find another envelope tucked inside. This one had a word puzzle on the front. Kevin's dad sat down at the table and worked on the puzzle.

"Close the door after you ___ ___ ___ ___ it. You mail a letter inside an ___ ___ ___ ___ ___ ___ ___ ___."

Kevin's dad opened the envelope. Out spilled a bunch of letters. He played around with them until he got the message: "There is another envelope hidden in your desk. Good luck finding it!" He looked and looked and finally found the envelope hidden among his unused envelopes. Inside were two pieces of paper. One was blank. The other said, "Look on the table in the family room. Take both pieces of paper with you."

On the table in the family room Kevin's dad found some watercolors and paintbrushes. There was an envelope that said, "Open before you paint." Inside was a rebus, which is a combination of words and pictures that spell out a message. Kevin's dad deciphered it. It said, "Paint the paper blue. You don't have to clean up the mess. P.S.: Please try not to be too messy. Thanks!"

Kevin's dad painted the paper blue. The words "go climb a tree" magically appeared. Kevin's dad climbed the tree in the backyard. Inside the tree house he found a box in the corner. When he opened it, he found a rolled-up piece of paper.

"A treasure map!" exclaimed Kevin's dad. "I haven't been on a treasure hunt in ages."

The directions said, "Find three prizes. The map has the clues. Do not open anything else. Come to the dining room with the prizes."

Kevin's dad searched until he had found the three prizes. One was hidden in the fort in the corner of the yard. He found the

BIBLE BANQUETS WITH KIDS

second one in the garden, and the third one was hidden under a cushion on a patio chair. He took all of the prizes to the family room. Kevin and his mom were waiting. While he was hunting, they had fixed his favorite breakfast for him.

"You can open the presents now," said Kevin. "Begin with the biggest box. Then open the narrow box. Open the square box last."

Inside the box was a piece of paper that said, "Wish Certificate. This certificate grants you the wish of a long walk in the woods, if you take Mom and me with you."

Next, his father opened the narrow box. There was another wish certificate: "This certificate grants you one long weekend camping trip in the mountains with your son, Kevin. We'll let Mom stay home since she hates camping."

The square box also had a wish certificate: "You have one more thing to find on your treasure hunt. This wish wears out soon, so you better look under your place mat fast."

Under the place mat was an envelope. A bunch of odd-shaped jigsaw puzzle pieces fell out. When put together they read, "Look behind the door." Behind the door was a giant-sized card. On the front it said, "Happy Father's Day to the bestest dad in the whole world."

Kevin's dad opened the card. Inside it said, "I'm really glad you are my dad. Thank you for helping me learn to do the right things. Thanks for playing with me and teaching me to ride my bike. Thanks for reading to me and telling me crazy stories. I love you. Your son, Kevin."

Kevin's dad gave him a great big hug. "It looks like we are going to have lots of fun together. Thank you for being such a good son. I'm a lucky dad!"

PUZZLE: *Who's Who?*

Can you find the names of these biblical fathers? Circle each name you find. The leftover letters spell out a message.

___ ___ ___ ___ ___ ___ ___ ___ ___ ___!

JOSEPH   GOD   ZEBEDEE
ABRAHAM   MOSES   ADAM
JACOB   ZECHARIAH   NOAH

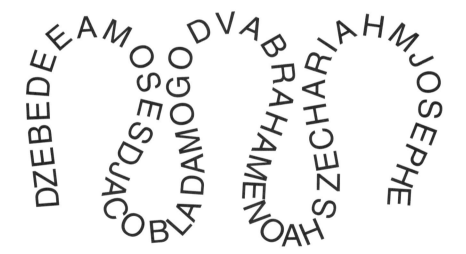

Use a piece of paper to create a Father's Day card for your dad. Draw a picture and write why you like having him for your dad. You can fold the paper any way you choose.

CHAPTER 12

Music Makers' Munchout

Have a musical year-end picnic for your children's choirs. Ask each choir to present one song. Take an instant photo of each child, director, and accompanist as they arrive. Label the back of the photo with the person's name. Set the photos aside for later in the program. An alternative is to ask people to bring a wallet-sized photo.

- ☐ **Theme:** Praising God for gifts of music

- ☐ **Memory Verse:** "Make a joyful noise to the LORD, all the earth; break forth into joyous song and sing praises. Sing praises to the LORD with the lyre, with the lyre and the sound of melody. With trumpets and the sound of the horn make a joyful noise before the King, the LORD" (Psalm 98:4-6).

- ☐ **Nametags:** Use the pattern on page 80 to make black cardboard musical eighth notes. Use red marker to print child's name on a white label and affix it to the note. Pin tag to child's clothes.

- ☐ **Food:** Hot dogs, chips, apples, cookies, and juice

- ☐ **Offering:** Ask each family to donate a children's music tape, to be given to an agency that works with children who have been abused or are in need. Provide a list of suggested titles (soundtracks from kids' movies, Bible songs, and so forth).

- ☐ **Table Decorations:** Locate music-themed table coverings, plates, cups, and napkins.

- ☐ **Room Setup:** An area where children can engage in musical activities, listen to stories, and create art projects. Weather permitting, have an outdoor picnic. Otherwise, have an indoor picnic on the floor.

- ☐ **Camera and Film:** Have an instant camera and film to take individual photos of the kids, their directors, and their accompanists.

MUSIC MAKERS' MUNCHOUT

PROGRAM

Welcome: "Let's Stand and Sing!" (Sung to "Pop Goes the Weasel")

Let's stand and sing
Our praises to God!
Let's clap our hands and sing.
And JUMP as we praise the Lord!

IDEA ✳

Sing it as a round.

Bible Stories: "Sharing Psalms" (Psalms 47, 100, and other favorites of your choice)

 Activity: A Psalm of Music (see page 78)

 Art: Instruments of Praise (see page 78)

 Game: Music Makers (see page 79)

 Project: Praise God for Our Music Makers (see page 79)

Recognition Ceremony: See page 80.

Grace: "Thank You, God" (Sung to "Twinkle, Twinkle, Little Star")

Thank you, God, for this food.
Thank you, God, for your love.
Thank you for our church and friends.

SOMETHING SPECIAL 🌀

Read the book *The Song* by Charlotte Zolotow.

Thank you for the chance to sing.
Thank you, God, for this day.
Thank you, God, for everything!

Munchout: Enjoy the picnic!

Closing: "Let Us All Praise the Lord" (Sung to "Mary Had a Little Lamb")

Let us go and praise the Lord, praise the Lord, praise the Lord!
Let us go and praise the Lord, for God's gift of music!
Let us sing and clap our hands, clap our hands, clap our hands!
Let us sing and clap our hands, for God's gift of music!

BIBLE STORIES
Sharing Psalms

Materials: sheet music of songs based on the psalms (Psalms 47, 100, and so forth); crayons; photos and/or drawings of things mentioned in Psalms; card stock paper; rubber cement; white paper; scissors

Directions
1. Explain that the psalms often become songs. Show examples of music that comes from the psalms.
2. Decide upon a creative way to share each psalm you choose.
   - If you decide to use story cards, draw pictures or have photos that illustrate the psalm. Use rubber cement to attach each picture/photo to a piece of card stock paper. Type the text and attach it to the back of the card. Number the cards so that the verses are in the correct order. Have kids stand in a line

and hold cards. Let each child read the back of the card as he or she holds up the picture or photo.
- Play rhythm instruments to highlight Psalms.
- Have kids do choral readings of the psalms. Divide the children into groups, and give each group a stanza. Print the stanza on cards for each person in the group. Color code the cards (stanza 1—blue, stanza 2—red, and so forth).

ACTIVITY
A Psalm of Music

Materials: chalk board or other easy-to-view writing surface

Directions

1. The kids are going to make up a musical psalm. The title will be "Let's Sing Our Songs of Praise to God" (Sung to "If You're Happy and You Know It").
2. Teach them this responsive line, which they will sing after each stanza.

> Let's sing our songs of praise to God! Let's sing our songs of praise to God!
> Let's sing our songs of praise,
> Let's sing our songs of praise,
> Let's sing our songs of praise to God!

3. Have each child think of one thing for which to praise God. Put those things to music. For example:

> Let's praise God for our food and homes! Let's praise God for our food and homes!
> Let's praise God, let's praise God, let's praise God, let's praise God!
> Let's praise God for our food and homes!

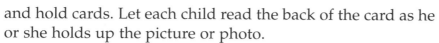

ART: Instruments of Praise

Materials: large and small heavy-duty cardboard paper plates; thin colored ribbons cut into 12-inch lengths; clean coffee cans with lids; plastic margarine tubs with lids; colored construction paper cut to fit cans; crayons; markers; rice; hole punch; glitter; glue; bells; yarn; lima beans

Directions

Let each child decide if he or she wants to make a drum, a shaker, or a tambourine.

Drums—Give each child a piece of colored construction paper and a coffee can. Tell the children to use crayons, markers, glue, and glitter to decorate it. Glue the paper to the can (the lid side up). You now have a drum.

Shaker—Let each child use glitter, sequins, and glue to decorate the margarine tub and lid. Fill it with rice, lima beans, or a combination of the two. Glue the lid to the tub. Let dry overnight before using.

Tambourine—Give each child one paper plate. Punch 10 holes around the outside edges, leaving open space at the sides. Give the kids 10 bells. Let them string the bells with the yarn and attach them firmly to the holes. The kids can decorate their plates with crayons, markers, glitter, and glue. Kids can add streamers by tying ribbons to the holes at the bottom. Let dry overnight before using.

GAME: *Music Makers*

Materials: 1 rhythm instrument per child; 1 conductor's baton (or small dowel rod); 1 large musical note per child; black poster board; clear contact paper

Prior to the Program

1. Use black poster board to make one large musical note per child (see page 80 for patterns). Cover the notes with clear contact paper.
2. Tape the notes to the floor, spacing them as far apart as possible.

Directions

1. Have each child stand on a note.
2. Clap your hands and have the children move about the room in time to your clapping. Experiment with different rhythms. Tell them to avoid stepping on the notes.
3. Stop clapping. Tell the children to find a note to stand on. Do this three times. After the third time, remove a note.
4. Have the kids move about in time to your clapping. Stop clapping and have the kids find a note to stand on. There will be one child without a note. Give that child a rhythm instrument. Remove another note.
5. Let the child play the instrument. Have the kids move about in time to the instrument. Have the child stop. Another child will be without a note. Have that child leave the game, and give him/her an instrument. Remove another note.
6. Now you will begin to conduct the band. Both kids will play in time to your conducting. Stop, and have the "marching kids" find a note.

NOTE ✳

This game is a great way to teach rhythm. It also helps kids learn to follow a conductor. In addition, all the kids are always occupied while the game is played.

7. The child without a note joins the band. Keep playing until everyone is in the rhythm band. If desired, have a couple of instrumental tapes for kids to play along with once they all become part of the band.

PROJECT
Praise God for Our Music Makers

The Bulletin Board

Materials: 1 large bulletin board covered with white paper, large musical notes cut from black paper (see patterns on page 80), other musical symbols (treble and bass clefs, fermatas, rests, and so forth); glue; scissors; stapler; red paper; individual photos of each child in the choir, the director, and the accompanist. (Use an instant camera or a school photo. Cut the pictures into circles so that they fit inside the notes.)

Prior to the Program

Use letter stencils to cut the following words out of red paper: "Praise God for Our Music Makers!" Staple the words to the bulletin board.

Directions

1. Put the musical notes into a large musical gift bag.
2. Let each child reach in and pick out a note.
3. Give each child his/her photo and glue. Tell them to glue their photos to their notes. Use these in the following Recognition Ceremony.

RECOGNITION CEREMONY FOR CHILDREN'S CHOIR

Materials: a tape of quiet, soothing instrumental music; 1 choir pin per child (These can be ordered from religious catalogs.); the musical notes with the kids' photos (Let kids hold these.); the bulletin board

Directions

1. Hold the ceremony near the bulletin board.
2. Form a circle with the kids. Have your accompanist stand in the circle too. Play the music tape. Teach the kids the response "We sing to the Lord!" Make sure your accompanist knows what to say and when to say it.

Director:	Praise the Lord for creating music and children to sing!
Children:	We sing to the Lord!
Director:	Thank you for creating composers who write music for these children to sing!
Children:	We sing to the Lord!
Director:	Thank you, God, for our accompanist ____ (name). Thank you for his/her dedication, patience, and love.
Accompanist:	Thank you, God, for allowing me this opportunity to serve you with music.
Children:	We sing to the Lord!
Director:	Thank you for our church and the opportunity to share our music with you and your beloved people.
Children:	We sing to the Lord!

3. Thank each child for being a part of your choir. If desired, say something special about each person. Then have the child go to the bulletin board and staple his/her note to it. Help them with placement as needed, so that it creates an eye-catching display. If desired, give each child a choir pin.

PUZZLE
A Musical Message

Write the correct note names under each note to spell out
a message. There are a couple of hints provided.

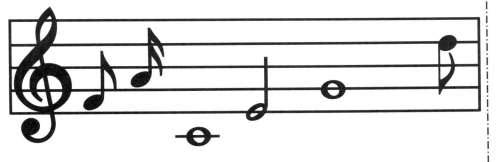

___ ___ ___ ___ ___ O ___

_ O R _ R _ _ _ _

PUZZLE
Where Do We Go?

Help the kids find their way to choir practice.

CHAPTER 13

Fourth of July Freedom Feast

Hold this program in connection with the Fourth of July weekend. Consider making this an informal, intergenerational worship service followed by a picnic. Play games and have fun celebrating our country's religious freedom.

☐ **Theme:** Thanking God for our freedom to worship.
☐ **Memory Verse:** "It is for freedom that Christ has set us free. Stand firm, then, and do not let yourselves be burdened again by a yoke of slavery" (Galatians 5:1 NIV).
☐ **Nametags:** Fourth-of-July-themed, self-stick nametags.
☐ **Food:** Picnic foods such as hot dogs; hamburgers; chips; cookies; red, white, and blue Jell-O salads; and lemonade. A large white sheet cake with red and blue sprinkles added to the batter, and white frosting. Use decorating gels or blueberries and raspberries to make the stars and stripes. Add numeral candles to indicate America's age.
☐ **Offering:** Ask each family or individual to bring a basket for a patient who is in a veterans' hospital. Baskets might include lotion; toothbrush and toothpaste; comb; soap; deodorant; shampoo; a paperback; and a puzzle book and pencil. Or consider providing several large baskets and having each person bring one item for the gift baskets.
☐ **Time:** 1½ to 2 hours
☐ **Room Decorations:** Red-white-and-blue banners and bunting. Display the U.S. flag, your state flag, and your denomination's flag. Look for red-white-and-blue centerpieces to put on white table coverings.
☐ **Costume Idea:** Have everyone dress in red, white, and blue. Ask an adult male to portray Jesus.
☐ **Field Trip Fun:** Arrange a field trip to a veteran's hospital. Take the baskets of goodies and sing patriotic songs with the patients.
☐ **Prior to the Event:** Appoint a committee to design a flag that represents your church. Hold a contest in which individuals and/or families can submit designs. Suggest that the symbols on the flag represent America and her freedom, your denomination, and your church. Once a design has been approved, ask volunteers to create the patterns and make the flag, which should be large, colorful, and attractive.

FOURTH OF JULY FREEDOM FEAST

PROGRAM

Welcome:

> **Leader:** We thank God for the freedom to worship Jesus.
>
> **All:** Praise God for the gift of freedom!

Song: "God Bless America"

Bible Story: "Jesus Gives the Great Commission" (Matthew 28:16-20).

Message: Have members of your congregation dress up as the Founding Fathers and tell how the United States of America was founded. Explain that religious freedom is one of our basic rights. Read the First Amendment of the United States Constitution: "Congress shall make no law respecting an establishment of religion, or free expression thereof." Explain that in some parts of the world people are not allowed to choose how they worship. Invite comments from participants. If people who have suffered religious persecution are in attendance, ask them if they are willing to share their stories.

Have Jesus enter and tell the story of giving the Great Commission (Matthew 28:16-20). Let Jesus tell that he wanted religious freedom for the world. Discuss how Jesus wanted us to share our faith with one another.

Show everyone the large sheet cake decorated like an American flag. Light the candles and sing "Happy Birthday" to America. You will enjoy this cake at the picnic.

The Story of Our Flags: Explain the meaning of the United States Flag. The stripes symbolize the original thirteen colonies. There is one star for each state of the union. Also discuss your state flag and denominational flag.

Our Church Flag: Present the flag that was designed to represent your church. Explain the meaning of the symbols in the flag, and display it in a prominent location.

Song: "You're a Grand Old Flag"

A Time of Sharing: Invite individuals to briefly share what living in America means to them.

Cheer: "America!" (see page 84)

Song: "America the Beautiful"

 Art: Flag Making (see page 85)

 Bulletin Board: God Bless America (see page 85)

Song: "This Land Is Your Land"

Closing:

> **Leader:** Let us go forth and celebrate our freedom.
>
> **All:** Let us share God's love with everyone!

CHEER: *America*

Materials: seven 12-inch square pieces of white paper; seven 12-inch square pieces of card stock paper; black marker; bright colored markers and crayons; rubber cement; large envelope; letter stencils

Prior to the Program

1. Use the black marker to outline the letters of "America" (one letter per sheet) on the seven sheets of white paper.
2. Color each letter with markers or crayons. You can use stripes, designs, swirls, and so forth.
3. Use rubber cement to mount the letters on the sheets of card stock paper.
4. Store the letters in the envelope with a copy of the cheer.

Directions

1. Have seven children form a straight line facing the audience. Give each child a letter. Show them how to hold it upside down, so that the letter faces them and cannot be seen from the audience. When they flip the letter up, it should be right side up and in view of the audience.
2. Do the following cheer. Ask another child to lead it by reading the "Leader" lines. Each "cheer leader" will hold a letter up high and shout it out. The rest of the kids and adults will make up the "cheering section."

AMERICA

Leader:	Give us an *A*!
Child 1:	*A! (Holds card high)*
Leader:	Give us an *M*!
Child 2:	*M! (Holds card high)*
Leader:	Give us an *E*!
Child 3:	*E! (Holds card high)*
Leader:	Give us an *R*!
Child 4:	*R! (Holds card high)*
Leader:	Give us an I!
Child 5:	*I! (Holds card high)*
Leader:	Give us a *C*!
Child 6:	*C! (Holds card high)*
Leader:	Give us an *A*!
Child 7:	*A! (Holds card high)*
Leader:	What does it spell?
All:	*America!*
Leader:	What does it spell?
All:	*America!*
Leader:	What does it spell?
All:	*America!*

ART: Flag Making
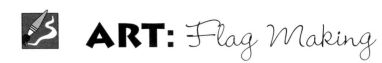

Materials: 1 piece of white muslin per family or individual (12 by 10 inches or larger); scraps of material; fabric markers and crayons; white paper; pencils; 1 long dowel rod per family or individual

Prior to the Program
Stitch down the left side of the piece of muslin, so that it makes a slot to slip the dowel rod through. It should be a snug fit.

Directions
1. Let families/individuals use the white paper, crayons, and markers to design a flag that represents them. Use the white paper for practice.
2. Have them draw their design on the muslin.
3. When finished, invite each family/individual to tell about their flag.

NOTE ✳

Have family members work together so that this becomes a true family project. Family members who wish to design individual flags can be encouraged to do so at home. Those people who are family-free can design a flag that represents them. It is important to be sensitive to the different kinds of life situations and family groupings in your church.

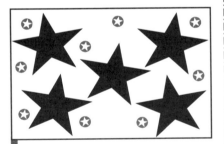

BULLETIN BOARD

God Bless America

Materials: white paper to cover bulletin board; thick black marker; thin-tipped red and blue markers; letter stencils; red and blue construction paper; scissors; stapler

Prior to the Program
1. Using the black marker, draw a large outline of the United States.
2. Trace the words "God Bless America" on red and blue construction paper. Cut the words out and staple them to the board.

Directions
1. Ask each person to use a blue or red thin marker to write a message to America inside the outline of the United States.
2. Post the outline on the bulletin board.

The Bulletin Board

PUZZLE
America the Beautiful

Complete the crossword puzzle below.
The shaded letters spell out a message.

Write it here: ___ ___ ___ ___ ___.
Then use colorful crayons to draw fireworks on your paper.

ACROSS:

1. The Declaration of
_____.
2. There were thirteen
_____ that
formed the United
States.
3. Thomas _____
helped write the
Constitution
4. From _____ to shining
sea.

DOWN:

1. Sweet land of _____.
2. In _____ we trust.
3. The _____
is the document that
governs the United
States of America.
4. _____ the
beautiful.
5. In the United States, we
have _____ of
religion.
6. There are fifty _____
on our flag.

PUZZLE
Blessings for America

Color: R=Red and B=Blue

CHAPTER 14

King Solomon's Feast

- ❑ **Theme:** Learning about wisdom from the wise acts of King Solomon.
- ❑ **Memory Verse:** "The LORD has kept the promise he made" (1 Kings 8:20*a* NIV).
- ❑ **Nametags:** Use the crown pattern on page 21.
- ❑ **Food:** A lavish potluck meal including salads, breads, soups, meat, desserts, and beverages
- ❑ **Offering:** Ask each child to bring a puzzle that someone his/her age would enjoy. This allows you to collect wooden preschool puzzles as well as more complex jigsaw puzzles for older kids. Donate these to an agency that works with children who have been abused or are in need.
- ❑ **Time:** 2 hours
- ❑ **Table Decorations:** Have fancy serving bowls and goblets. Use fancy paper table coverings, napkins, cups, and plates. Use tables that are close to the ground. Spread cushions on the floor for kids to sit on while they eat.
- ❑ **Room Decorations:** Decorate the room to look like the dining hall in King Solomon's palace (see Room Decoration Ideas, page 133). Provide an area where children can play games, work on art projects, and eat the meal.
- ❑ **Costume Idea:** Have a man portray King Solomon, and a woman portray the Queen of Sheba. The children and adults can dress up as members of King Solomon's court and as the people during biblical times.

Solomon, the third king of Israel, was a very wise man. He wrote Ecclesiastes, Song of Solomon, many proverbs, and some psalms. He learned that it is important to obey God. Encourage children to bring friends to this event.

KING SOLOMON'S FEAST
PROGRAM

Welcome: Welcome the kids and tell them you are going to learn about a very wise king. Have the person portraying King Solomon enter the room in royal dress. Act surprised as you greet him. Let him provide part of the welcome.

Bible Stories: Recount the stories of King Solomon (1 Kings 2–11, Ecclesiastes, Song of Solomon, Proverbs, and Psalms 72 and 127). Choose stories your children will enjoy. Ask King Solomon to share these stories. Invite the Queen of Sheba and members of King Solomon's court to share important happenings. Prior to the program, help the children decide what to share.

 Game: Wise Kids (see page 89)

 Bulletin Board: Do You Know? (see page 89)

Song: "Look How Smart He Is!" (Sung to "Pop Goes the Weasel")

> **SOMETHING SPECIAL**
>
> **Share one of these books with the children.**
>
> *The Wisest Man in the World* by Benjamin Elkin
>
> *The Flower of Sheba* by Doris Orgel
>
> *King Solomon and the Bee* by Dalia Hardof Renberg

They tried to trick the king,
But he was way too smart.
He answered all their riddles.
YES! He knew the answers!

Let the kids show how smart they are. They can create their own verses based on the "Something Special" story they just heard.

 Art: A Basket of Proverbs (see page 90)

Grace: "Thanks Be to God!" (Let a child lead this. Do it as a rap.)

Leader:	Thanks be to God.
All:	Thanks be to God.
Leader:	For giving us food!
All:	For giving us food!
Leader:	Let's share our blessings.
All:	Let's share our blessings.
Leader:	With everyone we meet!
All:	With everyone we meet!
Leader:	Amen!
All:	Amen!

Meal: Enjoy the feast!

Closing: "Give Us Wisdom" (Let a child lead this. Do it as a rap.)

Leader:	Please give us wisdom.
All:	Please give us wisdom.
Leader:	Let us use it wisely.
All:	Let us use it wisely.
Leader:	And do what's right.
All:	And do what's right.
Leader:	Amen.
All:	Amen.

GAME: Wise Kids

Materials: a large puzzle that depicts King Solomon (You will probably need to create one.); basket; glue; tape; markers; heavy poster board; card stock paper

The game will require a man dressed as King Solomon, and a woman dressed as the Queen of Sheba.

Prior to the Program

1. Use card stock paper to make the King Solomon puzzle. Draw the puzzle, color it, and cut out the pieces. It should be large (at least 3 feet square). You will need one piece per child. (It is better to have extra pieces than not enough.)
2. Trace the outline of the puzzle (including each piece) on a large piece of heavy poster board.
3. Put the puzzle pieces in the basket.

Directions

1. One at a time, each child can reach into the basket, pull out a puzzle piece, and take it to King Solomon. The Queen of Sheba will hold the basket.
2. King Solomon will take the piece, hold it to his head, and think hard. Then he will ask that child an age-appropriate question.
3. If the child answers the question correctly, the child can take the piece to the puzzle board and place it in the correct spot. Those who cannot answer the question must find someone who will help them learn the answer. Once they know it, they can return to King Solomon to tell him the answer and earn the privilege of adding a puzzle piece to the board.
4. Once the puzzle is completed, display it for all to see.

SAMPLE QUESTIONS

1. Who created the world? (God.)
2. What did God create on the fourth day of Creation? (Sun, moon, and stars.)
3. How many Commandments are there? (Ten.)
4. What is the second Commandment? (Worship only God.)
5. How does God want us to treat our parents? (Respect and obey them.)
6. Who built an ark and put animals on it? (Noah.)
7. What happened to Jonah when he disobeyed God? (He was eaten by a big fish.)
8. What kind of beautiful clothes did Joseph's father give him? (A multicolored coat.)
9. Which boy became a king at age 8? (Josiah.)
10. What baby was left in the bulrushes? (Moses.)

HINTS

1. You will need one question per child. Have a few extras in mind. Make a wide variety of age/ability-appropriate questions. It is okay to challenge the kids.
2. Older kids should be encouraged to look in the Bible for the answers they do not know. Help younger kids as needed.

BULLETIN BOARD
Do You Know?

Materials: religious symbols cut from colored construction paper (sun, star, dove, and so forth); scissors; stapler; push pins; clear contact paper; small folder; multicolored construction paper; colored construction paper; letter stencils; pencils; black felt-tip pens

Prior to the Program

1. Cover the bulletin board with multicolored construction paper.
2. Trace and cut out the title—"Do You Know?"—from colored construction paper and attach it to the board.
3. Cut out the symbols, using different colored pieces of construction paper. Make all of one shape the same color. (For example, the stars are blue, and the doves white.)
4. Create a list of proverbs that kids can use.

Directions

1. Let each child choose a proverb. Let them look through the Bible or your list. Or make it a game in which you have several proverbs written on individual slips of paper. Put them in a container and let the kids draw one.
2. Have the kids print proverbs on a shape. Help younger children as needed.
3. Cover each shape with clear contact paper, and let the kids cut off excess contact paper. Then have the kids cut the shapes in half.
4. Put one half of each proverb on the board.
5. Put the other halves into the folder. Attach the folder to the bulletin board. Put push pins along the bottom of the board.
6. Encourage children to see if they can match the proverbs. Encourage the children to invite adults to see if they can match the proverbs.

The Bulletin Board

ART
A Basket of Proverbs

Materials: 1 small berry basket per child; ribbons to fit through the slots on the baskets; card stock paper in a variety of colors; proverbs; rubber bands; crayons; pipe cleaners

Prior to the Program

1. Create and print a sheet of paper that contains 31 proverbs. Create a instruction sheet for using the Proverbs basket.
2. Copy the proverbs onto different colors of card stock paper.
3. Cut them out. Use rubber bands to bundle them into packets. Each child will get one packet containing all 31 proverbs.

Directions

1. Give each child a packet of proverbs. Let the children use crayons to draw a border around each proverb. Caution them not to cover the words, since the words must be easy to read.
2. Let the kids weave the ribbon through the berry basket. Attach a pipe cleaner to make a handle.
3. Let the kids put their proverbs into their baskets.
4. Send home a sheet of instructions that encourages parents to select one proverb a day to read and discuss with their children.
5. For extra fun encourage kids to memorize 31 proverbs. At the end of the month, those kids who can recite 31 proverbs can be invited to a pizza party with the pastor.

PUZZLE: *Wisdom*

Look in your Bible (NRSV) to find the missing words to these proverbs.

1. For the LORD gives wisdom; from his mouth come
◯_ _ _ _ _ _ _ _ and understanding (Proverbs 2:6).
2. Trust in the LORD with all your heart, and do not rely on your own
_ _ _◯_ _ _ (Proverbs 3:5).
3. My child, do not forget your teaching, but let your heart keep my
_ _ _ _ _ _ _ _ _◯_ _ (Proverbs 3:1).
4. Hear instruction and be wise, and do not _ _◯_ _ _ _ it
(Proverbs 8:33).
5. A _ _◯_ child loves discipline, but a scoffer does not listen to
rebuke (Proverbs 13:1).
6. A soft answer turns away wrath, but a harsh _◯_ _ stirs up
anger (Proverbs 15:1).
7. The eyes of the◯_ _ _ are in every place, keeping watch on the
evil and the good (Proverbs 15:3).
8. The light of the eyes _ _ _◯_ _ _ _ the heart, and the good
news refreshes the body (Proverbs 15:30).
9. _ _ _◯_ _ your work to the LORD, and your plans will be
established (Proverbs 16:3).
10. The human mind plans the way, but the _◯_ _ directs the steps
(Proverbs 16:9).
11. The◯_ _ _ of the LORD is a strong tower; the righteous run into
it and are safe (Proverbs 18:10).
12. To◯_ _ _ _ over mouth and tongue is to keep out of trouble
(Proverbs 21:23).
13. Apply your mind to instruction and your _◯_ to words of
knowledge (Proverbs 23:12).
14. My child, give me your heart, and let your _ _ _◯observe my
ways (Proverbs 23:26).
15. Every◯_ _ _ of God proves true; he is a shield to those who
take refuge in him (Proverbs 30:5).

16. Listen, _ _◯_ _ _ _ _, to a father's instruction, and be
attentive, that you may gain insight (Proverbs 4:1).
17. Lying lips are an abomination to the LORD, but _ _ _◯_ who
act faithfully are his delight (Proverbs 12:22).
18. Whoever walks with the _ _ _◯becomes wise (Proverbs
13:20*a*).

Print the circled letters here. What's the message?

_ _ _ _ _   _ _ _ _ _ _ _   _ _ _   _ _ _ _.

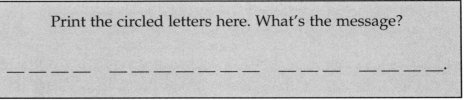

PUZZLE
A Crown Fit for a King

Trace the dotted lines. Then use crayons, glue, and glitter to
decorate King Solomon's crown.

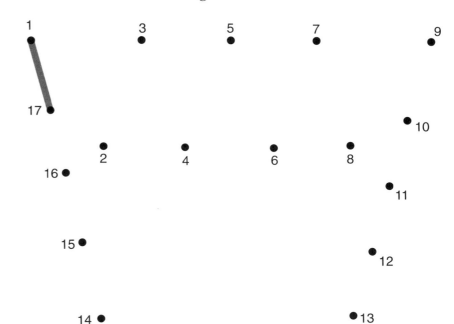

CHAPTER 15

A Bread Basket Breakfast

This program can be held in connection with World Wide Communion Sunday, which is celebrated by Christian churches all over the world on the first Sunday in October. Have a Bread Basket Breakfast at which you talk about how bread came to be used for our Holy Communion meal. Consider holding the program prior to morning worship to help the children learn about the Sacrament of Communion, and then allow them to receive Communion at the worship service. Have parents attend with their children. Let this be an intergenerational program.

❏ **Theme:** Learning about Holy Communion and World Wide Communion Sunday

❏ **Memory Verse:** "Then he took a loaf of bread, and when he had given thanks, he broke it and gave it to them, saying, 'This is my body, which is given for you. Do this in remembrance of me'" (Luke 22:19).

❏ **Nametags:** Use the loaf of bread pattern on page 96.

❏ **Food:** Have a light breakfast featuring a variety of breads from around the world; fruits; and grape juice.

❏ **Offering:** Ask each child to bring a box of crackers or breadsticks. Give these to the local food pantry.

❏ **Time:** 1 to 1½ hours

❏ **Room Decorations:** Have a large globe and maps of the world. Put push pins into the countries where your church denomination is located. Find large, colorful photos of children from other lands. Decorate an area to resemble the Upper Room where Jesus and his disciples shared the Last Supper. Set up the "Bethlehem Bakery" in the kitchen or teaching area. Have an authentic-looking sign and an arched entrance into the bakery. Create scenery that resembles an old oven and place it in front of the oven in the kitchen.

❏ **Costume Idea:** Dress as Bethlehem bakers, wearing tunics and baker hats.

❏ **Field Trip Fun:** Arrange a field trip to a local bakery to see how they make bread.

A BREAD BASKET BREAKFAST

PROGRAM

Welcome: Welcome everyone, and explain that you are going to learn about a very special celebration and Sunday—Holy Communion and World Wide Communion Sunday. Tell the children that Christians all over the world will take Communion today and that World Wide Communion Sunday brings us together in Christian unity.

What is Communion anyway? In simple terms, explain the ritual of Holy Communion according to your church teachings.

 Activity: Bread Making

Bible Story: Tell the story of the Last Supper (Matthew 26:17-75; Mark 14:12-42; Luke 22:1-62; John 13:1-38).

 Bulletin Board: God Loves Kids All Over the World (see page 94)

 Art: Bread Dough Crosses (see page 95)

Grace: "Let Us Share This Meal" (Sung to "Michael, Row the Boat Ashore")

Let us share this meal together, Alleluia.
Let us share God's love, Alleluia.

Meal: Share a meal of bread, fruits, and juices.

Worship and Communion: Have the children participate in the worship service. Work with the pastor and other worship leaders to make this an intergenerational worship service that relates to World Wide Communion Sunday. Ask your children's choir to sing a Communion anthem. "We Come to Your Table," from *High God 2*, is an excellent selection. Have the adult choir sing a Communion anthem as well.

Explain that we eat nutritious foods so that we can have healthy bodies, which allow us to work and play well. Tell people that taking Communion gives us the spiritual strength to do God's work in the world. Sing songs such as "Let Us Break Bread Together," "One Bread, One Body," and "Eat This Bread."

Share an intergenerational message that speaks about the importance and significance of World Wide Communion Sunday. You can use bread that the children make this morning. Let the children "serve" Communion to the congregation.

> ### SOMETHING SPECIAL 🌀
>
> **Choose any of these books to share with the children.**
>
> *Everybody Bakes Bread* by Norah Dooley
>
> *Bread Is for Eating* by David and Phillis Gershator
>
> *Loaves of Fun* by Elizabeth M. Harbison
>
> *Knead It, Punch It, Bake It!* by Judith Jones
>
> *Bread, Bread, Bread* by Ann Morris
>
> *All About Bread* by Geoffrey Patterson
>
> *Bread* by Dorothy Turner

 **ACTIVITY:** *Bread Making*

Materials: mixing bowls, packaged bread mix, cookie sheets, preheated oven

1. Have the children make and bake extra loaves of bread to use for Communion. Put the loaves into bread baskets, and set them in the sanctuary. Tell the congregation, that the morning's Communion bread was baked by the children.
2. Let the children experience the different parts of bread making. Have corn and wheat for them to grind with millstones. Let them add water to the powdered dough mixture and mix it until it becomes doughy. Explain that this is how people made bread in biblical times.

Prior to the Program

1. Mix the bread dough so that it is ready to use in time for the program.
2. Let the bread dough sit and rise.

Directions

1. Give each child a large hunk of dough. Let the children knead and mold their bread into any shape they choose. They can braid it, roll it into breadsticks, make small loaves, and so forth.
2. Put the loaves of bread on large cookie sheets. Make note of where each child's piece of bread is. Bake the bread according to the directions on the box.
3. Serve it warm.

BULLETIN BOARD
God Loves Kids All Over the World

Materials: Large bulletin board covered with light blue paper; black construction paper; large cutout of the world; photos of children from around the world, and the children in your church (Ask kids to bring a photo from home or take an instant photo.); stapler; letter stencils; scissors

Prior to the Program

1. Cover the bulletin board with blue paper.
2. Staple the world cutout to the center.

3. Trace the title "God Loves Kids All Over the World" onto black paper. Cut out the letters and staple them to the bulletin board.
4. Cut out the photos of kids from different countries. Use rubber cement to attach them to colored pieces of construction paper. Use a black marker to print the names of the countries under the correct pictures. Put the photos in a large basket.

Directions

Have each child take turns reaching into the basket, pulling out a picture, then putting their picture on the bulletin board. Staple the picture to the board for each child.

The Bulletin Board

GOD LOVES KIDS ALL OVER THE WORLD

(Sung to "Paw Paw Patch")

Refrain:

God loves kids all over the world!
God loves kids all over the world!
God loves kids all over the world!
God loves you and me!

Verse:

As each country is added, change the verses to highlight that country.

God loves the kids in Africa!
God loves the kids in Africa!
God loves the kids in Africa!
God loves kids all over the world!

When all the pictures are up on the board, sing the refrain again. Now it is time to add the photos of your children. Sing the same tune and use the names of your children.

God loves Robert, Emily, and Cathy!
God loves Kyle, Angie, and John!
God loves Sarah, Rachel, and Tommy!
God loves the kids right here in our church!

Do this until all the kids are named and added to the board. For fun, have the kids add pictures of one another rather than their own. Then sing the refrain one last time.

ART
Bread Dough Crosses

Materials: play dough (see recipe); cross-shaped cookie cutters; rolling pins; one 24-inch piece of leather string per child; flour; pencils and black markers; newspapers; 1 small piece of cardboard per child; glitter; sequins; and glue

Prior to the Program
Make several batches of play dough and store it in air-tight containers until time for use.

Directions
1. Give each child a piece of play dough. Show them how to roll it out so that it is smooth and even.
2. Let each child use a cross-shaped cookie cutter to cut a cross out of the play dough. Kids can decorate these with glitter, sequins, and glue, if desired, or leave them plain.
3. Use the eraser end of the pencil to poke a hole in the top of the cross.
4. String the leather cord through the hole and tie it at the top.
5. Tell the children to let these dry for a couple of days before wearing them. Lay each cross on a piece of cardboard and label with the child's name. Tell the children to turn the cross over tomorrow, so that the other side can also dry.

RECIPE ✳

Mix 1 cup of flour, 1 cup of salt, and 1/2 cup water. Add small amounts of extra flour or water to get the proper consistency. Makes about 10 to 15 crosses.

PUCLE...

PUZZLE
World Wide Communion Sunday

1=A	5=E	9=I	13=M	17=Q	21=U	25=Y
2=B	6=F	10=J	14=N	18=R	22=V	26=Z
3=C	7=G	11=K	15=O	19=S	23=W	
4=D	8=H	12=L	16=P	20=T	24=X	

Use the above letters to decode the sentence below.

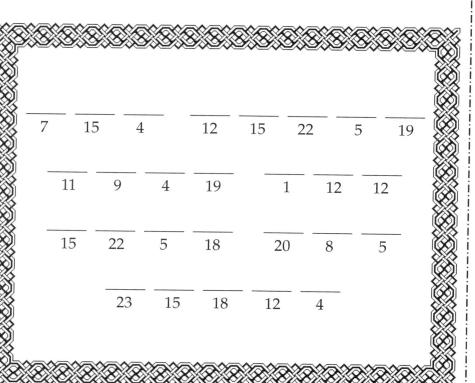

```
___ ___ ___   ___ ___ ___ ___ ___
 7   15   4   12   15   22   5   19

___ ___ ___ ___   ___ ___ ___
11    9    4   19    1   12   12

___ ___ ___ ___   ___ ___ ___
15   22    5   18   20    8    5

___ ___ ___ ___ ___
23   15   18   12    4
```

PUZZLE
Somebody Loves You

Color: R=Red, O=Orange, Y=Yellow

Bread Pattern for Nametags

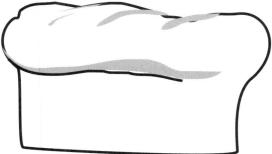

BIBLE BANQUETS WITH KIDS

CHAPTER 16

Feed One Another Brunch

❑ **Theme:** Sharing food with others

❑ **Memory Verse:** "I was hungry and you gave me food" (Matthew 25:35*a*).

❑ **Nametags:** Use food-shaped self-stick nametags.

❑ **Food:** Have a biblical meal with fish (fish sticks, shrimp, and so forth), fruits, bread, juice, and cookies.

❑ **Offering:** Several weeks prior to this program, give each family/individual a brown grocery bag with the words "Feed One Another" written on it. Ask them to fill the bags with non-perishable foods as a donation for a local food pantry. Borrow some shopping carts from a local grocery store and collect the donations. Ask people to also donate coupons that can be used in local food stores.

❑ **Time:** 1½ to 2 hours

❑ **Table Decorations:** Use food-related table coverings, plates, cups, napkins, and globes for centerpieces.

❑ **Room Decorations:** Paint a backdrop of a tree and an outdoor scene. Put a large piece of artificial grass on the floor in front of the scene. Place a rock or tree stump on the grass. Have an area where kids can work on art projects, play games, and eat.

❑ **Costume Idea:** Ask an adult to dress as and portray Jesus.

Hold this program in connection with World Food Day on October 16. Invite all members of your congregation to attend.

FEED ONE ANOTHER BRUNCH
PROGRAM

Welcome: Let a child lead this.

> **Leader:** God, we thank you for providing food for the world.
> **All:** Let us share your food with the world.

Story: "Feed One Another" (see page 99)

Song: "Let's Share Our Food"
(Sung to "The Bear Went Over the Mountain")

> Let's share our food.
> Let's share our food.
> Let's share our food.
> With all of the world.
> With all of the world, with all of the world.
> Let's share our food.
> Let's share our food.
> Let's share our food.
> With all of the world!

Bible Story: "I Was Hungry" (Matthew 25:31-40). Invite a person to portray Jesus and to tell this story to the children. Let him explain that God puts enough food on this planet for everyone, and that God wants us to share the food we have with people who do not have enough to eat. Discuss how we can do that. Jesus can relate this story to "Feed One Another," presented earlier in the program.

 Game: Grocery Shopping (see page 100)

 Bulletin Board: Let's Share Our Food (see page 101)

 Art: Grace Plates (see page 102)

Grace: "Come Say 'Thank You'" (Sung to "Frere Jacques")

> Come say "Thank you!"
> Come say "Thank you!"
> For this food!
> For this food!
> God gives us many blessings!
> God gives us many blessings!
> We love God!
> We love God!

Once the children know this, let them sing it as a round.

Meal: Enjoy the brunch.

Closing: "Let Us Share" (Let a child lead this.)

> **Leader:** Let us share our blessings with other people.
> **All:** Let us praise the Lord by sharing! Amen.

BIBLE BANQUETS WITH KIDS

STORY: Feed One Another

Materials: 8 yardsticks or 3-foot-long dowel rods with plastic spoons attached to one end by rubber bands; small oyster crackers inside 3 baskets

Ask a woman to play the Angel, and a man to play the Man.

Directions

1. Ask one of the older classes (fourth/fifth grade or junior high) to assist with the story. The program leader should act as Narrator.
2. Divide everyone into two groups of six to eight people. Have one group sit on the far left, and the other on the far right. The actors will "freeze" when they are not part of the discussion. Place a basket of oyster crackers in the middle of each group. Give half of the people in each group a dowel rod with a spoon attached.
3. Have the Angel sit alone center stage and freeze. Put a dowel rod with a spoon attached and a basket of oyster crackers next to her in view of the audience.
4. Have the dowel rod with spoon lying on the ground (not in use) next to the group on the right.

5. Let the kids take turns feeding one another with the dowel rods with spoons. Then let the kids reenact the story.

Tell the story.

Narrator:	One day a man died and began his journey to heaven. On the way, he was stopped by an angel.

The Angel and the Man move to center stage. Both groups freeze.

Angel:	God has some special plans for you. But first God wants me to ask you what ideas you have for eternity.
Man:	I don't care where I go. I don't believe in heaven and hell. Just take me to a place where I will have enough to eat. And I don't want to share, either.
Angel:	Okay, as you wish.

The Angel takes the Man to the group on the left. They should begin to try and eat with their long utensils. However, they cannot because the utensils are too long. The food falls on the floor.

Man:	What's going on here? These people aren't getting enough to eat!
Angel:	God always provides enough to eat.
Man:	I don't like this place. Take me somewhere else!
Angel:	As you wish.

The group on the left goes into "freeze action." The group on the right begins movement. Their utensils are identical; however, they are feeding one another. The Angel and Man walk over to the right side of the stage.

Angel:	Here we are.
Man:	What's going on? What are they doing?
Angel:	They are doing what God wants us to do. They are making sure that everyone has enough to eat.
Man:	Take me to another place.
Angel:	Sorry, there are only two places to go.
Man:	These are my choices?
Angel:	These are your choices.

The man looks around and sees a woman sitting all alone. She looks hungry and lonely. There is a dowel rod with spoon, and a basket of crackers sitting next to her.

Man:	Who is that? Why does she look so sad?
Angel:	She just arrived too. She hasn't decided where she wants to go, either.

The man looks around thoughtfully. He walks over to the right side of the stage, picks up the long spoon and a handful of crackers. He goes and sits down across from the woman and offers to feed her. She accepts. She reaches down, picks up another long spoon, puts some crackers on it and offers to feed the man. He accepts. They both walk to the right side of the stage where they sit down among those who are feeding one another. The people on the right side resume action when the man and woman join them. Discuss this scene with the children.

GAME: *Grocery Shopping*

Materials: box fronts from a variety of food boxes; labels from canned goods

Prior to the Program
Hide the box fronts and labels throughout the building. (Hide the box fronts/labels for each age group in a different room or area. This allows you to control the difficulty level.)

Directions
1. Assign each age group to a different room where things are hidden, and tell each child to look for three items.
2. After they find three items, tell them to go to the bulletin board, where they will help assemble the display on the board.
3. Talk about the different kinds of food items they found. Ask, Why do we eat these foods?

BULLETIN BOARD
Let's Share Our Food

Materials: 1 large bulletin board covered with colored paper; the box fronts found in the Grocery Shopping game; stapler; photos of kids from around the world; brightly colored construction paper; glue sticks; scissors; letter stencils

Prior to the Program

1. Use letter stencils to trace the words "Let's Share Our Food" out of brightly colored construction paper. Cut them out and staple them to the board.
2. Glue the pictures of children from around the world to the bulletin board.

The Bulletin Board

Directions

Let each child have a turn putting the food items on the board. Help the children, as needed, with placement and stapling. While this is going on, sing the following song:

LET'S SHARE OUR FOOD

(Sung to "Mary Had a Little Lamb")

Let's share our food with everyone, everyone, everyone.
Let's share our food with everyone
All over the world.

Add verses that go with the food items you are adding to the board.

Let's share our cereal with everyone, everyone, everyone.
Let's share our cereal with everyone
All over the world.

ART: Grace Plates

Materials: 1 large heavy-duty paper plate per child; pencils; markers; glue; pictures of food cut from magazines; blank writing paper; 1 envelope per child

Prior to the Program

1. Cut out 5 to 10 food pictures for each child. Include a variety (dairy, meat, grains, desserts, beverages, soups). Put the pictures in individual envelopes.

2. Precut one piece of paper per child. It should fit inside the paper plate.

Directions

1. Give each child a piece of paper, and tell the children to create a table grace that they can use at home with their families. Help kids, as needed, with printing, spelling, and grammar. Keep in mind that some kids (especially younger children) will need help composing a grace. Make sure each child's name is on his/her grace plate.

2. Have kids glue their grace to the inside of the paper plate.

3. Give each child an envelope of pictures. Tell the kids to glue these to the other side of their plates.

4. Children can take them home to use when they say grace at meals.

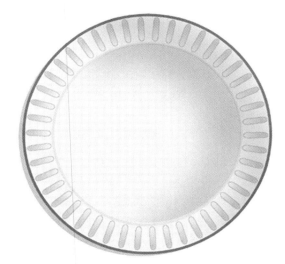

PUZZLE
What Should We Do?

Unscramble the words inside each cloud. Color B=Blue.

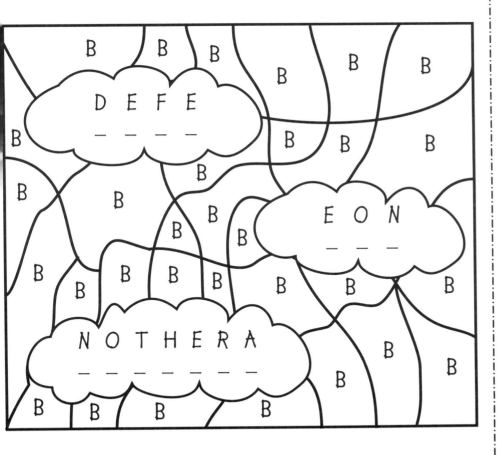

PUZZLE
How Can We Help?

Color B=Blue, G=Green, R=Red, O=Orange, P=Purple, Y=Yellow

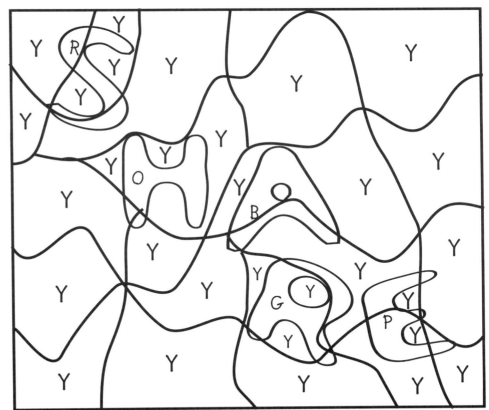

CHAPTER 17

A Bountiful Blessings Banquet

This program is ideal for Thanksgiving. Invite all members of your congregation, and let the children host the event. Instruct the children on how to politely greet and welcome their guests and to serve the meal. Arrange seating so that there is a mix of children and adults at each table. The children can create room and table decorations.

☐ **Theme:** Giving thanks for our bountiful blessings.

☐ **Memory Verse:** "Let us come into his presence with thanksgiving; let us make a joyful noise to him with songs of praise!" (Psalm 95:2).

☐ **Nametags:** Use Thanksgiving or autumn-theme self-stick nametags.

☐ **Food:** Have a Thanksgiving banquet consisting of turkey, stuffing, vegetables, fruits, breads, and desserts. Have a variety of juices for the beverages.

☐ **Offering:** Ask each family/individual to bring one family meal made up of nonperishable foods (for example, large family-sized box of macaroni and cheese, canned fruits, and cookies; or large can of soup, crackers, and pudding). Collect the donations in a grocery cart, then take them to a food pantry.

☐ **Time:** 2 hours

☐ **Table Decorations:** Find attractive Thanksgiving table coverings with matching napkins, plates, and cups. The children can create Thanksgiving centerpieces. Use orange votive candles inside candleholders.

☐ **Room Decorations:** Adorn the walls with autumn posters, leaf cutouts, Thanksgiving decorations, and the children's creations. Provide an area where people can sit and listen to stories (chairs for adults, floor for kids), tables and chairs to work on projects, and tables and chairs for the meal.

A BOUNTIFUL BLESSINGS BANQUET
PROGRAM

Welcome: (Let a child lead this.) Welcome your guests and tell them that you are going to have a time filled with God's blessings of love and goodness.

Song: "Thank You, God, for Bringing Us Together" (Sung to "Paw Paw Patch")

> Thank you, God, for bringing us together.
> Thank you, God, for bringing us together.
> Thank you, God, for bringing us together.
> Let's give our thanks to God.
>
> Let's give our thanks to God our Creator.
> Let's give our thanks to God our Creator.
> Let's give our thanks to God our Creator.
> Let's give our thanks to God!

Psalm 95: Make this into story cards. Print the appropriate text for each verse on the back of the card. Use photographs or pictures drawn by children. Show the pictures as you read the psalm.

 Project: Psalms of Thanksgiving (see page 106)

Song: "We Gather Together"

 Game: Cornucopia of Blessings (see page 107)

Story: "Sharing Thanksgiving" (see page 109)

 Art: Thanksgiving Turkey (see page 107)

Entertainment: Let the children provide a variety show. Invite the children's choir to sing a Thanksgiving song, the preschool and kindergarten classes to share a Thanksgiving fingerplay, and other classes to present a short puppet show or a brief skit.

Grace: "Let's Give Thanks for Our Food" (Say it as a rap, with clapping and snapping. Have a child lead it.)

Leader:	Let's give thanks for our food.
All:	Thank you, God, for our food. Amen! Amen! Amen! Amen!

Meal: Enjoy the banquet.

Closing: "Let Us Share" (Let a child lead this.)

Leader:	Let us share God's blessings with everyone we meet.
All:	Let us share God's love with the world. Amen.

> **HINT** ⊙
>
> If time is needed to reset the tables for the meal, plan to show a Thanksgiving-related video or a Bible story video. Have several adults and older children reset the tables during this time. Arrange the tables for the dinner in a large U-shape, with people seated on both sides. Then continue with your program.

PROJECT
Psalms of Thanksgiving

Materials: 1 piece of lined notebook paper per family/individual; one 8½-by-10-inch piece of white paper per family/individual; crayons; pencils; 9-by-13-inch sheet of orange construction paper per family/individual

Directions

1. Give each family or individual a piece of notebook paper. Tell people to create their own Thanksgiving psalm.

2. Give each group or person an 8½-by-10-inch sheet of white paper. Tell them to illustrate their psalm.

3. Have them fold the sheet of orange construction paper in half and decorate the outside of it. Tell them to write the psalm title on the cover and then glue the psalm and illustration inside the booklet.

4. Ask each family/individual to read their psalms of Thanksgiving aloud and show their illustrations.

My
Thanksgiving
Psalm

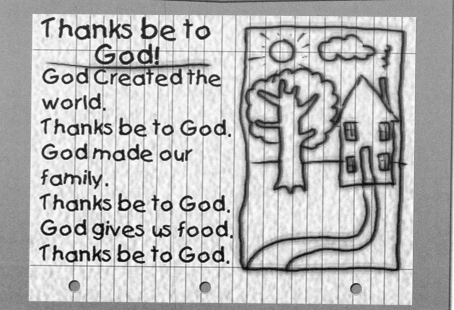

Thanks be to God!
God Created the world.
Thanks be to God.
God made our family.
Thanks be to God.
God gives us food.
Thanks be to God.

GAME
Cornucopia of Blessings

Materials: 1 extra large cornucopia (found in craft stores); 1 of each of the following items: small toy, book, mittens, can of soup, picture of a house, picture of a car, pictures of friends, church picture directory (or photo of your church); 1 bag of Hershey's Kisses chocolates; 1 bag of Hershey's Hugs chocolates

Prior to Program

Put the Hugs and Kisses in the bottom of the cornucopia. Place the rest of the items on top (in any order you choose).

Directions

1. Ask another adult to hold the cornucopia on his or her lap and to sit next to you, while the kids sit on the floor in front of you.

2. Explain that we have a cornucopia of blessings and that we are going to give thanks for all of the blessings we have. Have everyone say, "Let's thank God for all of our blessings!" (Do it as a rap, alternating clapping hands and snapping fingers with each syllable.) Explain that we will say that response after each item is removed and shown.

3. Ask one child to stand, to close his or her eyes, pull the top object out of the cornucopia, and hold it up high. Keeping with the rhythm, the child will say, "Thank you, God, for our _____ (name item)!"

4. The other children will respond, "Let's thank God for all of our blessings!" Keep playing until only the Hershey's Kisses and Hugs are left.

5. When you get to the Hugs and Kisses, ask the children what they remind them of. (Love.) Explain that God gives us all of these blessings because he loves and cares for us. Tell the children that God wants us to share our love and God's love with everyone. Discuss how we show our love to our parents, friends, and other people. Tell them that there are enough Hugs and Kisses for each of them to have one of each. Then give them a second Hug and Kiss to share with one of the adults. As the kids give the candy away, they can say "God loves you."

ART: *Thanksgiving Turkey*

Materials: 1 large turkey (Enlarge pattern on page 108 to fit your bulletin board.); sponges (small round or square shaped); thick, dark brown tempera paint; newspapers; colored, thin felt-tipped markers (red, purple, dark blue, and dark green work best); letter stencils; scissors; stapler; green, blue, yellow, and orange construction paper; tape

IDEA ✳

Make smaller copies of the turkey pattern, and let the children make their own turkeys to take home. These can be cut out and mounted on blue construction paper. Encourage parents to frame them.

Prior to Program

1. Cover the table with newspapers. Put paint into pie tins. Set sponges next to them.

2. Use tape to secure the turkey to the table.

3. Use blue paper to make the sky, and green paper to make hills. Put them on the bulletin board. Make the sun from yellow paper and add it to the bulletin board.

4. Use letter stencils to trace the words "Our Bountiful Blessings" on orange paper. Cut it out and staple it to the bulletin board.

Directions

1. Talk about all of the blessings we have in our lives (home, school, books, friends, clothes, food, and so forth).

Pattern

2. Let each child use a colored marker to write one of his/her blessings inside the turkey's feathers.

3. Have each child take turns sponge painting the turkey's body with brown paint.

4. Let dry. Cut out the turkey and hang on the bulletin board.

BIBLE BANQUETS WITH KIDS

STORY: *Sharing Thanksgiving*

Make this into a flannel board story. Trace the patterns onto the pellon (purchase at fabric store), color them, and cut them out. If desired, you can add a scented sticker to the back of each piece, so that the children can smell the different foods. Be sure to make the pieces large and colorful. Ask the children to join in on the repetitive phrase "That basket sure smelled good!"

Rocky Raccoon and Hoppy Hare were playing in the woods. "I wonder how Scamper Squirrel is doing," said Rocky Raccoon.

"I haven't seen her since before she broke her leg," said Hoppy Hare. "It's sad that she can't go visit her friends for Thanksgiving. I wish there was something we could do to help her."

"You know what?" said Rocky Raccoon. "I think we can help her." Rocky whispered something in Hoppy Hare's ear. Hoppy nodded enthusiastically and hopped off.

The next day was Thanksgiving. Rocky and Hoppy met by the old tree just as they had planned.

"Did you bring it?" asked Hoppy Hare.

"I sure did!" said Rocky Raccoon. "The turkey is all cooked, and it's in this big basket." "I made the stuffing. I'll just put it in the

basket," said Hoppy Hare. "Won't Scamper Squirrel be surprised when we show up with Thanksgiving dinner?"

"That basket sure smelled good!"

Rocky started walking toward Scamper's house. Hoppy hopped along next to him. Soon they met Carla Cardinal. She was sitting on a low tree branch singing.

"Hey, where are you going with that big basket?" asked Carla Cardinal.

"We're taking Thanksgiving dinner to Scamper Squirrel. She broke her leg," explained Rocky.

"Can I come? I just picked a bunch of berries," said Carla.

"Sure, put them in the basket," said Hoppy.

"That basket sure smelled good!"

Rocky walked, Hoppy hopped, and Carla flew overhead. "Ribbit, ribbit, ribbit," sang Frisky Frog. "Hey, where are you going?" he asked.

"We're taking Thanksgiving dinner to Scamper Squirrel. She broke her leg," explained Rocky Raccoon.

"Can I come?" asked Frisky Frog. "I have some tasty oranges I could bring."

"Sure, put them in the basket," said Hoppy.

"That basket sure smelled good!"

Rocky walked, Hoppy hopped, Frisky leaped, and Carla flew overhead. They had to go through a field to get to Scamper Squirrel's tree house.

"Hey, where are you all going? asked Handsome Horse.

"We're taking Thanksgiving dinner to Scamper Squirrel. She broke her leg," explained Rocky Raccoon.

"Can I come?" asked Handsome Horse. "I have an apple pie we could have for dessert."

"Sure, put it in the basket," said Hoppy Hare.

"This basket is getting heavy!" exclaimed Rocky Raccoon.

"I'm getting tired of hopping," said Hoppy Hare.

"I'm getting tired of flying," said Carla Cardinal.

"I'm getting tired of leaping," said Frisky Frog.

"In that case, climb on my back, and I'll give you a ride. Attach the basket to me. I'll carry it," said Handsome Horse.

The animals were having a great time riding on Handsome Horse's back. Soon they came to a stream.

"Hang on, I have to cross the stream," said Handsome Horse.

They heard someone crying. It was Quacker Duck.

"Why are you crying, Quacker?" asked Carla Cardinal.

"Because I don't have anyone to spend Thanksgiving with. I have to spend it all alone," she quacked.

"No you don't," said Frisky Frog. "You can come to Scamper Squirrel's with us. She broke her leg, and we are taking Thanksgiving dinner to her."

"Can I come, can I really come?" cried Quacker Duck. "I have some crackers I could bring."

"Sure, put them in the basket around Handsome Horse's neck," said Hoppy.

"That basket sure smelled good!"

"Find a place on my back," said Handsome Horse.

Quacker Duck put her food in the basket and climbed up on Handsome Horse's back.

Soon they came to Scamper Squirrel's tree house. They knocked on the door.

"Come in," called Scamper sadly.

The animals all tumbled into Scamper's tiny tree house.

"Where did you all come from?" Scamper cried in surprise.

"We brought Thanksgiving dinner!" said her friends.

"What a wonderful surprise! *That basket sure smells good!*" exclaimed Scamper.

Scamper told her friends where to find the tablecloth, the plates, and the cups. They set a beautiful Thanksgiving table. They all sat down around the table.

"Let's say grace," said Scamper.

"Thank you, God, for giving me such good friends. And thank you for all of this delicious food!"

"Amen!" said her friends.

"That food sure tasted good!"

BIBLE BANQUETS WITH KIDS

PUZZLE: *Thanksgiving Message*

If you color all of the Xs brown, you will have a Thanksgiving message. Print the message in the spaces at the bottom. Inside the feathers write some of the blessings you have.
Color your turkey and decorate your paper.

__ __ __ __ __ __ __   __ __   __ __ __

__ __ __ __   __ __ __ __ __ __ __

__ __ __ __!

Look in your Bible. What psalm is this from?

_____

X	G	X	X	X	X	X	X	I	X	X
X	V	X	X	E	X	X	X	T	X	X	X	H
X	X	A	X	X	N	X	X	X	K	X	X	X
S	X	X	T	X	X	O	X	T	X	X	X
X	X	H	X	X	E	X	X	X	X	X	X	L
X	O	X	X	R	X	D	X	X	X	F	X	X
X	X	O	X	X	R	X	X	G	X	X	X	O
X	X	D	X	X	I	X	S	X	X	G
X	X	O	X	O	X	D	X	X

PUZZLE
Turkey of Thankfulness

Trace the dotted lines. Color B=Blue, G=Green, R=Red, O=Orange, Y=Yellow, P=Purple. Write (or ask someone to help you write) a Thanksgiving message inside the turkey's body.
Color it light brown when you are finished.
Mount your turkey on a piece of colored construction paper. Ask Mom or Dad to frame it and hang it up. It can become a permanent Thanksgiving decoration.

CHAPTER 18

Christmas Cookie Cookfest

Hold this program during Advent. Ask the parents to bring several batches of homemade sugar cookie dough to the program, or prepare several batches of your favorite. The dough must be the consistency to be rolled and cut with cookie cutters. Provide decorating sprinkles and gels. Parents and children can attend this event together.

☐ **Theme:** Learning the meaning of Christmas symbols. Sharing gifts with others.

☐ **Memory Verse:** " 'Do not be afraid; . . . I am bringing you good news of great joy for all the people' " (Luke 2:10).

☐ **Nametags:** Use self-stick Christmas nametags.

☐ **Food:** Snack on freshly baked Christmas cookies and hot chocolate.

☐ **Offering:** The children will bake and package several batches of cookies to be donated to your local fire department. You can ask parents and children to drop these off after the program. You can also ask each child to bring a bag of cookies to be donated to the local food pantry.

☐ **Table Decorations:** Locate Christmas-themed tablecloths.

☐ **Room Setup:** Set up tables where children can make cookies and ornaments, as well as provide an oven where cookies can be baked.

CHRISTMAS COOKIE COOKFEST

PROGRAM

Welcome: Ask one of the children to lead this.

Leader: The bells of Christmas ring out, reminding us of Jesus' love.

All: Let us rejoice in Jesus' love!

Bible Story: Matthew 1:18–2:12 and Luke 2:1-39. Make a flannel board of the Christmas story and share it with the children.

Song: "O Come, All Ye Faithful"

 Game: Find the Cookie Cutters

 Activity: Cookie Making and Baking (see page 114)

 Bulletin Board: A Christmas Quilt (see page 114)

Story: "What Does It Mean?" (see page 115)

 Art: Play Dough Christmas Ornaments (see page 117)

> **SOMETHING SPECIAL** 🌀
>
> **Read one of these stories to the children.**
>
> *The Legend of the Poinsettia* by Tomie dePaola
>
> *The Candymaker's Gift* by David and Helen Haidle
>
> *The Legend of the Candy Cane* by Lori Walburg

Grace: (Let a child lead this.)
Jesus, thank you for being our loving Savior. Let us share your love with everyone we meet. Thank you for letting us share these cookies with one another and with our friends at the fire department. Amen.

Meal: Feast on freshly baked cookies and hot chocolate.

Closing: (Let a child lead this.)

Thank you, God, for sending us Jesus. Help us share your love with everyone. Amen.

Let each child take home his/her ornaments and two Christmas cookies. Put the other cookies on Christmas plates and deliver them to the neighborhood fire department that serves your church. Be sure to tell the firefighters and paramedics that the kids baked the cookies for them. Attach a note to each batch delivered: "Thank you for keeping us safe. Merry Christmas from the children at _____ (church name)." Include your church address and phone number.

> **HINT** 🌀
>
> Call the fire department and ask how many workers are on each shift. Send two cookies per person. Ask one of the families in your church to deliver the cookies.

GAME
Find the Cookie Cutters

Materials: 1 cookie cutter per child; a large Christmas cookie tin

Prior to the Program
Hide the cookie cutters.

Directions

1. Tell the kids that it is time to make the Christmas cookies.
2. Open the tin. Express surprise at finding an empty tin by saying, "Well, the cookie cutters were in here this morning. I saw an elf hiding here this morning. He didn't know I saw him. I bet he hid the cookie cutters. I guess we are going to have to look for them. I want each of you to look around and see if you can find one cookie cutter. When you find it, please bring it to me and put it in the tin."
3. When all of the cookie cutters are found, continue with the program.

HINT

If you are working with a multi-aged group, hide the cookie cutters for each age group in a different location. This allows you to adapt the difficulty level of the hiding places.

Hide cookie cutters for young children in easy-to-find locations. Older children can be challenged with more difficult hiding places.

ACTIVITY
Cookie Making and Baking

Materials: each child's 2 to 3 batches of sugar cookie dough (or the cookie dough you prepared); rolling pins; cookie sheets; cooling racks; large Christmas-themed paper plates for cookies; plastic food wrap; flour; note cards; decorating sprinkles, and gels; work table; nonstick pan spray

Ask each person to bring one rolling pin, cookie sheet, and cooling rack.

Directions

Have parents and children work together.

1. Give each parent and child the batch of cookie dough they brought. Have them cut out several cookies and lay them on a sprayed cookie sheet. Cover the cookies with sprinkles.
2. Label each sheet of cookies with the family's last name, and bake.
3. Remove cookies from the oven, let them cool a few minutes, then place them on cooling racks.

BULLETIN BOARD
A Christmas Quilt

This bulletin board design accommodates 24 children. If you have additional children, make additional quilts and display them on the walls. If you have fewer, let adults create squares so that you have 24 finished squares.

Materials: (Adapt the sizes given here to fit your bulletin board space.) 1 large bulletin board (about 55 by 37 inches) covered with red-and-green patterned Christmas wrapping paper; one 8-inch square sheet of white construction paper per child; several cookie cutters in the following shapes: candy cane, bell, star, Christmas tree, and wreath; red and green powdered tempera paints; 1 paintbrush per color; newspapers; red and green thin felt-tip marker; pie tins for the paints; rubber cement; spatulas

Prior to the Program

1. Put two heaping tablespoons of tempera into each pie tin. Add a small amount of water and mix. Paint should be quite thick. Stir with a spatula.
2. Cover the tables with newspapers.
3. Cover the bulletin board with the Christmas wrapping paper.

Directions

1. Give each child a piece of white construction paper. Let the children choose the cookie cutters they want to use.

2. Have each child dip the cookie cutter into the paint tin. Show children how to press the cookie cutter to the paper and lift it quickly, so that it leaves a print. (Do not move cookie cutters around on the paper. Cookie cutters should be dipped in one color only.) Let kids create their own designs, and use red or green markers to autograph their prints. Let dry.

Making the Bulletin Board

1. Staple the squares to the bulletin board, leaving borders around each.
2. Create signs that explain the meaning of each Christmas symbol. Hang the signs next to the bulletin board.
3. Encourage the congregation to look at the bulletin board the kids created.

The Bulletin Board

Provide a small Christmas tree. Have each of the following ornaments: angel, star, candy cane, wreath, Christmas tree, bells, candle, poinsettia, and holly. The ornaments are added as the story is told.

An alternative is to create a flannel board story. Use green felt to make a Christmas tree. Put the tree on the flannel board. To create the ornaments, lay pellon over a picture of a symbol and trace. Color the symbols with crayons, then cut them out. Put them on the tree as you tell the story.

"Mom, what does 'the symbols of Christmas ornaments' mean?" asked Gloria, reading the box as she put it on the living-room table.

"I've had those ornaments since I was a little girl. Every year in Sunday school we made a different ornament. Each one helped tell us about Jesus," said Mrs. Andrews as she opened the box.

"Oh, I made this Christmas tree when I was in kindergarten," said Mrs. Andrews. "Every year in Sunday school we made a new ornament to put on it. *(Hold up Christmas tree)* It reminds us of the everlasting love of Christ. It also reminds us that if we welcome Christ into our hearts, we will have his everlasting love." *(Put tree on table or flannel board)*

"Let's sit down and I'll tell you about the ornaments," said Mrs. Andrews.

"Now you know about the Christmas story," said Mrs. Andrews. "Long, long ago a woman named Mary was visited by an angel *(Hold up angel)* named Gabriel, who told her that God had chosen her to give birth to his Son, Jesus. Mary was very surprised, but she was pleased that God had chosen her. The angel also visited Joseph to tell him the same news. You see, Joseph and Mary were planning to get married, and the angel wanted both of them to know that God chose them to be the earthly parents of Jesus.

"One day they had to go to Bethlehem to register for the census. So Mary and Joseph traveled to Bethlehem. Mary rode the donkey while Joseph led the way on foot. Soon, it was time for the baby to be born. Joseph asked the innkeeper if they could have a room.

"'I'm sorry, all of our rooms are full,'" said the innkeeper.

"'But my wife is about to have a baby, and we need a place where he can be born,'" said Joseph.

"'All I have is some room in the stable. I'll show you where it is,'" said the innkeeper.

"Joseph followed the innkeeper to the stable. Behind him walked the donkey with Mary riding on it.

"Joseph made a bed of hay for Mary to lie on. Then he found a manger, which is really a feeding bin for the animals. He filled it with hay and set it next to Mary. He lit the candles in the lanterns. Soon Mary gave birth to the baby. It was a boy, and they named him Jesus.

"When Jesus was born, a huge star (*Hold up star*) appeared in the midnight sky. The star let people know that Jesus had been born in the stable. The shepherds in the fields saw the star and were terrified. But an angel (*Hold up angel*) appeared to them and told them not to be afraid. The angel told them to follow the star to Bethlehem, where they would find the baby. (*Put angel on tree*) They followed the star, and do you know what? They found

Baby Jesus lying in a manger in the stable. His parents, Mary and Joseph, were sitting next to him looking at him the way new parents look at a new baby. The shepherds knelt and prayed. (*Put star on tree*) The star also led the Wise Men to baby Jesus. We made this star in first grade. My first-grade teacher, Miss Henderson, gave each of us an angel ornament to add to our collection.

"Now, each shepherd had a staff. This was used to help keep the sheep where they were supposed to be. But many years later, a candymaker decided to use it to teach children about Jesus. (*Hold up candy cane*) The candy cane is shaped just like a shepherd's staff, if you hold it up like this. But if you hold it like this (*Turn it over*) it looks like a J for "Jesus." The candy is hard—to help us remember how solid God's love for us is. It is white to tell us that Jesus was without sin. The large red stripe reminds us of Jesus' blood that will be shed on the cross. And the three narrow red stripes remind us of the Trinity—God the Creator, Jesus the Son, and the Holy Spirit. The candy is sweet, which helps us remember the gentle love Jesus has for us. I remember making the candy canes in second grade. (*Put candy cane on tree.*)

"Here's a small wreath ornament. We made these in third grade. (*Hold up wreath*) The wreath is green to remind us of Christ's everlasting love. It's round to remind us that we always have a circle of love around us. (*Put wreath on tree*)

"I remember when we made these bells in Sunday school. That was the year I was in fourth grade. (*Hold up bells*) Bells are used to call people to church. (*Put bells on tree*)

"And my Christmas candle. I made that in fifth grade. (*Hold up*

candle) Candles remind us that Christ was born by candlelight. It also reminds us of the enlightenment Jesus brings to our lives. (*Put candle on tree.*)

"And here's the poinsettia. This is from sixth grade. (*Hold up poinsettia*) It looks like it has red flowers all over it, but those are really the leaves. Legend says the leaves on this plant turned red the night Jesus was born. (*Put poinsettia on tree*).

"Oh, we made this holly ornament when I was in seventh grade. (*Hold up holly*) A holly wreath looks like the crown of thorns that was placed on Jesus' head when he was crucified. The red berries remind us of his blood. Now, many people think of holly as bringing us good luck and good health." (*Put holly on tree.*)

"What did you make in eighth grade?" asked Gloria.

"That was the year I was confirmed. We had to use our tree and ornaments to tell the Christmas story to one of the younger classes in Sunday school. That was lots of fun!

"Well, Gloria, these are the stories about the Christmas symbols and how I came to have them."

"Wow, that's way cool, Mom!" said Gloria.

IDEA ✳

Let the children take two of their ornaments home, leaving the others at church. Use them to decorate the church's Christmas tree.

ART
Play Dough Christmas Ornaments

Materials: several batches of play dough; cookie cutters (star, candy cane, Christmas tree, wreath, bell, star); large plastic food storage bags; white self-stick labels; paper plates; newspapers; pencils with erasers; red and green 6-inch strands of yarn; small rolling pins

Prior to the Program

1. Make the play dough: Mix 1 cup flour, 1 cup salt, and ½ cup water. Add additional flour and water until you have the desired consistency. Add green powered tempera or food coloring to one batch, red to another batch, and leave one batch white. You may need more than three batches of dough, depending on the size of the group. One batch makes 10 to 15 ornaments.
2. Have each colored batch in a separate container.

Directions

1. Give each child and parent a piece of play dough. Use the rolling pins to roll the dough, so that it can be cut.
2. Have the children use the cookie cutters to cut out play dough cookies. Let the children glitter their cookies. Use a pencil eraser to punch a hole in each cookie. String cookies with yarn.
3. Put each child's cookies on a paper plate. Cover with plastic food storage bag. Print each child's name on a label and attach it to the plastic bag.
4. Tell kids to remove the plastic bag and let the cookies dry over night. The kids can hang the cookies on their Christmas trees.

PUZZLE: *Christmas*

Unscramble these words. Print them in the spaces provided. What do the circled letters spell? _____

TARS	YOHLL	DYCAN NEAC
SLEBL	DACNLE	MASCHRIST REET
LANGES	THREAW	SETTPOINIA

PUZZLE
Christmas Decorations

Trace the dotted lines. Color your Christmas decorations.

BIBLE BANQUETS WITH KIDS

CHAPTER 19

Happy Birthday, (church name)! Banquet

□ **Theme:** Celebrating your church's birthday (anniversary).

□ **Memory Verse:** "Go therefore and make disciples of all nations, baptizing them in the name of the Father and of the Son and of the Holy Spirit, and teaching them to obey everything that I have commanded you" (Matthew 28:19-20a).

□ **Nametags:** Use a computer to print people's names on self-stick tags.

□ **Food:** Have a potluck meal that includes appetizers, main dishes, salads, fruits, vegetables, breads, desserts, and beverages. Also, provide "kid favorites" such as peanut butter and jelly; fried chicken; and macaroni and cheese. Ask a local bakery to create a large sheet cake with a picture of your church or your denomination's logo on it and the words "Happy _____ (year) Birthday, _____ (church name)!" This can be one of the desserts.

□ **Offering:** Collect a special offering and use the money to purchase a special gift for the children's program (rug, puppets, and so forth).

□ **Time:** 2 hours

□ **Room Decorations:** Use balloons, streamers, and confetti. Let the kids create some of the decorations. Invite them to make centerpieces and to draw on white, paper table coverings.

Find out when your church was established and plan a birthday celebration. Plan a special celebration for a milestone birthday (10, 25, 30, 50, 75, 100, and so forth). There are many things you and the children can do to help celebrate this special day in the life of your congregation. Begin planning at least a year in advance. Think of a theme that represents your congregation and highlight it as part of your celebration. Invite former pastors and their families, and former members to share in this special day. The program is intended as a intergenerational program for children, their parents, and members of the church. Let the kids host the event. Consider offering this program as part of your worship service on the day you celebrate your church's birthday, or offer it as a separate program at another time.

IDEAS ✳

Think of something special you would like to do to commemorate your church's birthday. Would you like to add a stained-glass window that depicts one of the Bible stories featuring children? Is there something your church really needs? Maybe you would like to purchase a large area rug for the children's Christian education area, or the altar where the kids sit for the children's sermon. Perhaps you would like to purchase a large-screen video projector for Family Film Nights or for showing videos as part of Christian education. Think of a unique way of earning money to purchase your gift.

Pennies from Heaven: Get a large glass jar and put it in a prominent place. Have the kids make "penny banks" from margarine containers. Give each child a margarine container, and let them decorate it. Use a sharp knife to slice an opening through the plastic lid. Let each kid take the penny bank home and fill it with pennies. When the bank is full, the kids can bring it to church, empty it into the large jar, and start saving pennies again. You can also have them approach the congregation on Sunday mornings and ask for pennies. At the end of the year of your celebration, count the pennies, then use them to purchase something special for your children's program (books, room decorations, special materials and supplies, and so forth).

Pen Pals: Does your denomination have churches in other parts of the world? If so, choose a church and start a Pen Pals Club. Exchange pictures of your church and its members, Sunday bulletins, and newsletters. Encourage each class to make connections with a class or with individuals in the other church. An option is to choose a church in another part of the country. You might even be able to communicate via E-mail or fax. Make this an ongoing project.

Puzzles: Make a book of puzzles about your church, the Bible, Jesus, and so forth. Include crossword puzzles, word searches, dot-to-dots, mazes, word paths, scrambled words, and coloring puzzles for all ages. Consider including a few pictures to color. Enlist an artist to help with the drawings and design. Make an eye-catching cover. Give one book of puzzles to each child.

Magnets: Produce several hundred refrigerator magnets with your church's name, address, and phone number printed on them. Give one to each adult who attends your birthday celebration. Use the remaining supply as gifts for visitors to your church, which is a good way to encourage them to visit again.

HAPPY BIRTHDAY, _____ (CHURCH NAME)! BANQUET

PROGRAM

Welcome: Happy birthday! (Let a child lead this.)

Leader:	Happy birthday, _____ (church name)!

All:	We praise God for being able to celebrate your birthday, and for being able to worship God in such a great church. Amen.

Our Church: Prior to your celebration, enlist a member to write a true story about your church. Add humor, and make it enjoyable for all ages. Read the story aloud. Print copies for the people to keep, and to put with church history files.

Song: "We Are the Church" by Richard K. Avery and Donald S. Marsh (no. 558 in *The United Methodist Hymnal*)

Bible Story: Invite the pastor to tell the children how Jesus' disciples began the Christian church. Use the Memory Verse as the basis and explain that Jesus told the disciples to go out and share his teachings with the world. That was the beginning of the Christian church.

Bubble Prayers: Give everyone a jar of bubbles. Begin with an opening prayer that thanks God for your church. Then let people offer individual prayers about your church and its ministries as they blow bubbles. For example: "Thank you, God, for our children's choir." "Praise God for the preschool program that runs during the week." "Thanks be to God for our Parents' Day Out Program."

 Project: A Wall of Remembrance (see page 122). Have a dedication ceremony.

Special Music: Get a local composer to write an anthem for the children to sing for the program. Suggest that the song talk about the children's ministries. Let the kids sing this for your celebration. Or write new lyrics for a well-known tune that is in the public domain. Talk about your church and its offerings.

 Game: Church Trivia (see page 122)

 Art: Sign On (see page 123)

Song: Sing some of your congregation's favorite hymns.

Affirmation Ceremony: (see page 124)

Grace: (Let a child lead this.)

> Creator God, thank you for helping create our church. We like it a lot! Thank you for being with us as we celebrate our ____ (year) birthday. Let us celebrate many more birthdays. And, thank you for this delicious food that we are going to eat. Amen.

Meal: Have the food tables set up, and the older children to act as servers.

 Bulletin Board: Our Birthday, Our Future. (see page 124)

Closing: (Let a child lead this. Do it as a rap.)

Leader:	Thank you, God! Thank you, God! Thanks for our church!

All:	Thank you, God! Thank you, God! Thanks for (church name)!

PROJECT
A Wall of Remembrance

Materials: 1 large blank wall; photos of current church members, former members, and former pastors/staff and their families; writing paper; pens and pencils; letter stencils; large binder; see-through sleeves for binder

Directions

1. Contact former pastors/staff and their families and former members and their families. Ask them to write a letter sharing some of their favorite memories of your church. Tell them you are especially interested in the memories of their children and the children's programs. These letters might include humorous events, baptisms, marriages, and things that happened in worship, on retreats, and in classes. Ask that they include a current photo. Invite the current staff to submit letters and photos also.

2. Create a "Wall of Remembrance." Ask an artist in your congregation to design an eye-catching sign. Put the letters and photos on the wall for all to enjoy. Dedicate the wall, using your own words, as part of the program.

GAME
Church Trivia

Materials: trivia questions; prizes (pencils, pens, erasers, magnets, and other items with the church's name, address, and phone number on them); a bag; color-coded containers

This game will require a moderator.

Prior to the Program

1. Establish a committee to create trivia questions about your church. For example, What year was this church established? What year did we move into this building? Who was our first pastor? What is the name of our current pastor's dog (or cat)? What was the name of our first pastor's wife/husband? What is the name of our current pastor? Be sure to include questions for kids and adults. Consider color coding the questions (for example, yellow index cards for adults, blue index cards for children, and green index cards for teens), and put the cards in separate color-coded containers.

2. Put prizes in a bag.

Directions

Use a game-show setup with three contestants and a moderator. Each "game-show guest" wins a card if they answer correctly. If they cannot answer, the question goes to the next guest on the right. If that person answers correctly, he or she gets the card. At the end of five rounds, the guest with the most cards wins a special prize. Think of other ways to play this with your group.

 **ART:** *Sign On*

Materials: 1 piece of 9-by-12-inch white construction paper per child; one piece of 9-by-12-inch card stock paper per child; crayons; 1 paint stick per child; pencils; glue; clear book tape

Directions

1. Give each child a piece of white construction paper, crayons, and pencils. Ask them to create a sign that highlights your church (music, Sunday school, VBS, and so forth).

2. Use rubber cement to attach the construction paper to the cover stock paper. This will make the sign sturdy.

3. Attach the sign to the paint stick, using book tape.

4. Have a parade so that the kids can show off their signs.

IDEA ✳

1. Let kids make practice signs on scratch paper.

2. Older kids can make larger signs if desired. You will need a dowel rod or garden rod for mounting large signs.

3. Let the kids use these for the Affirmation Ceremony (see page 124).

4. Consider allowing the children to march in a city or town parade, carrying their signs.

AFFIRMATION CEREMONY

Materials: 1 colored votive candle (various colors) in a glass holder per person; 1 large white candle; 1 long tapered candle

Directions

1. Gather everyone and perform the affirmation ceremony. Let an older child be the leader.
2. Place the votive candles on the altar.

> **Leader:** God, we are so thankful for our church.
> **All:** Praise God for _____ (church name).
> **Leader:** One at a time, we will use the taper to light one of the colored candles on the altar. As we light the candle, we will give thanks for something we really like about our church.

Each person lights a small, colored votive candle and says, "God, I give thanks for. . . ." Have the children create an affirmation that highlights the sign they just made. They can hold it up as they light the candle.

> **All:** Praise God for _____ (church name)!

After all the candles are lit, continue.

> **Leader:** Thank you for all of our members and for all the work they do.
> **All:** Praise the Lord! Praise the Lord! Praise the Lord! Amen.

Song: "Blest Be the Tie That Binds" (verse 1)

BULLETIN BOARD
Our Birthday, Our Future

IDEA ☀

Give each adult a pen and/or a magnet with your church's name, address, and phone number printed on it. Give each child a church pencil and a puzzle book.

Cover your bulletin board with pastel colored paper. Make a large birthday cake with one candle for each year. On each candle, print one of the ministries of your church. Use an instant camera to take photos of kids and put the photos in the center of the cake. Add a sign that reads, "Our Birthday, Our Future."

The Bulletin Board

PUZZLE: *A Special Place*

Connect the dots to make a special place. Color B=Blue, G=Green, R=Red, O=Orange, P=Purple, Y=Yellow.

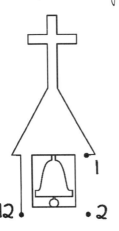

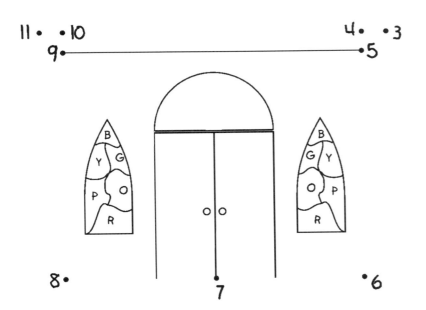

PUZZLE: *Going to Church*

What will we say when we go to church today? Decipher the code to find out! _____

1=A	5=E	9=I	13=M	17=Q	21=U	25=Y
2=B	6=F	10=J	14=N	18=R	22=V	26=Z
3=C	7=G	11=K	15=O	19=S	23=W	
4=D	8=H	12=L	16=P	20=T	24=X	

Use the code above to create a puzzle that reads "Happy Birthday, _____ (church name)." The "Happy Birthday" is already done for you. Make this one subtraction facts.

CHAPTER 20

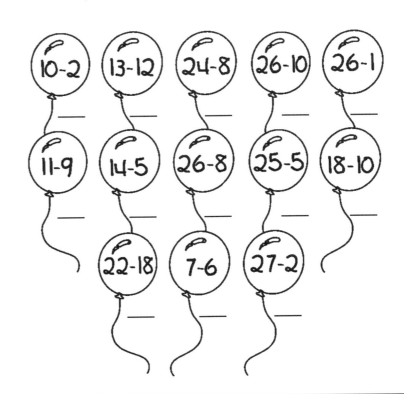

Welcome to Our New Church: A Potluck Celebration

This program celebrates the opening of a new or renovated church building, or the forming of a new congregation. Consider holding it on the first Sunday you worship in your new/renovated building or meet as a new church. The program can complement a weekly worship service or be held as a separate event. This can be for the entire congregation. Let the children act as hosts.

During a building program, let every child have the opportunity to buy a brick for $1. Have a nameplate with the child's name and age as well as the year the building or addition was dedicated. Have a brick wall made up of the children's bricks. Title the wall "Our Wall of Faith" or "Our Church's Strong Foundation." This allows the children to contribute to building the church.

Take photos of the entire building process. Include photos of people studying the blueprints; the empty construction site; the bulldozers clearing and digging; the empty hole; the foundation; the walls going up; and the roof being put on. Include photos of the inside process as well. At the end, have photos of the finished building.

For new congregations, take photos of your first worship service, including a snapshot of each person or family group. Begin a scrapbook that includes photos and bulletins. Ask a historian to begin compiling a history of your congregation.

☐ **Theme:** Celebrating a new building or a new congregation. Consider developing a special theme that highlights your congregation (such as "Reaching Forward, Reaching Upward, Reaching Onward!").

☐ **Memory Verse:** "Trust in the LORD forever, for in the LORD GOD you have an everlasting rock" (Isaiah 26:4).

☐ **Nametags:** Use self-stick nametags.

☐ **Food:** Have a potluck meal; ask families and individuals to bring food items. If desired, look for scriptures that highlight the foods you bring.

☐ **Offering:** Collect an offering that will be used to purchase a special item for your new building or congregation.

☐ **Time:** 1½ to 2 hours

☐ **Table Decorations:** Let the children use crayons and markers to decorate paper table coverings. Add such items as hammers, nails, screwdrivers, bricks, and hard hats.

☐ **Room Decorations:** Enlarge photos taken during the construction process. Put them on the walls. Provide an area where people can play games, make projects, and eat.

WELCOME TO OUR NEW CHURCH: A POTLUCK CELEBRATION

PROGRAM

Welcome: "Praise the Lord for Our Church" (Do it as a rap. Let the children lead the adults through it.)

Praise the Lord for our church!
Praise the Lord! Praise the Lord! Praise the Lord!
Praise the Lord!
Yes, Praise the Lord!
Praise the Lord!
Praise the Lord for our church!

Let the kids think of movements (clapping, snapping, stamping, jiving, and so forth). Once kids know it, see how fast they can say it.

Bible Story: "The Wise Man and the Foolish Man" (Matthew 7:24-27, Luke 6:46-49)

Change the house in the scripture to a church. Have two men dramatize this story for the children, telling it in their own words. Then discuss what happens when we do not make our church buildings strong and safe. Explain that our faith must be strong too. If we have a strong faith, we can cope with the difficulties that life brings. If we do not have a strong faith, life's difficulties can overwhelm us.

You could do this as a pulpit drama during worship.

Song: "Building a Church" (Sung to "The Wheels on the Bus")

The foolish man built a church upon the sand, a church upon the sand, a church upon the sand.
The foolish man built a church upon the sand, and the church stood straight and tall.

A big storm came, and the wind blew hard (*whoosh!*), the wind blew hard (*whoosh!*), the wind blew hard (*whoosh!*).
A big storm came and the wind blew hard (*whoosh!*), and rain fell all around.

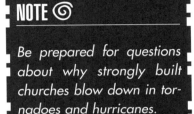

> **NOTE** Be prepared for questions about why strongly built churches blow down in tornadoes and hurricanes.

All of a sudden the church blew down, to the ground, to the ground. All of sudden the church blew down and it went ker-splat! (*Clap hands*)

The wise man built a church upon the rock, a church upon the rock, a church upon the rock.
The wise man built a church upon the rock, and it stood straight and tall.

A big storm came and the wind blew hard (*whoosh!*), the wind blew hard (*whoosh!*), the wind blew hard (*whoosh!*).
A big storm came and the wind blew hard (*whoosh!*), and rain fell all around.
The church stood strong and didn't fall, didn't fall, didn't fall. The church stood strong and didn't fall; it stood straight and tall.

 Art: Banner Making (see page 128)

Story: "This Is the Church That We Built" (see page 129)

 Bulletin Board: Open the Doors and See All the People (see page 130)

Game: A Church Treasure Hunt (see page 131)

Grace: "Praise God for Our Food" (Do it as a rap. Let a child lead it.)

Praise God for our food, for our food, for our food, for our food! Praise God for our food! Yeaaaaaaaaah, GOD!

Meal: Enjoy the potluck feast.

Closing: "Thanks Be to God!" (Let a child lead this.)

Thanks be to God!
Thanks be to God!
Thanks be to God for our church and for our people!
Thanks be to God!
Thanks be to God! Aaaaaaaaaamen!

 # ART: *Banner Making*

Materials: 2 long light-blue felt banners (6 by 3 feet); letter stencils (12 inches high); colorful felt (red, blue, green, purple, orange, bright pink, bright yellow); scissors; fabric glue; felt shapes (sun, butterfly, cross, and so forth) in a variety of colors; two 3½-foot dowel rods; mountings to hang the banners

Prior to the Program
1. Use the letter stencils to trace the words "Welcome Friends" onto felt. Vary the colors.
2. Install the wall mountings in a prominent place so that banners greet all who enter.

Directions
Let the children decorate the banners with words and felt shapes.

Use fabric glue to attach the felt to the banners. One banner should read "Welcome," and the other "Friends." Slip dowel rods through banners and hang them from wall mountings.

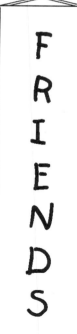

STORY
This Is the Church That We Built

Materials: blueprints of your church building; bricks and other building materials (shovels, cement, trowels, windows)

Directions

Take the kids on a tour of the building. Invite the children to join in on the refrain "for the church that we built."

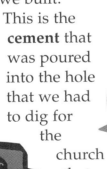

These are the **blueprints** for the church that we built. These are the **shovels** that were used to dig the hole that we had to dig for the church that we built.

This is the **dirt** that was in the hole that we had to dig for the church that we built.

This is the **cement** that was poured into the hole that we had to dig for the church that we built.

These are the **bricks** that we used for the walls of the church that we built.

These are the **nails** that we pounded into the walls of the church that we built.

These are the **hammers** that we used to pound the nails into the walls of the church that we built.

These are the **windows** that we put in the walls so that we could see outside of the church that we built.

These are the **doors** we put in the walls so that we could get in and out of the church that we built.

These are the **chairs (pews)** that we put in the church so that we could sit down in the church that we built.

Keep going, and then end with this last line:

This is the place where we come to worship the Lord. This is the church that we built!

BULLETIN BOARD
Open the Doors and See All the People

Materials: 1 large bulletin board; white paper; colored construction paper to match your church exterior; stapler; photos of people in your church engaged in activities

Prior to the Program

1. Cover the bulletin board with white paper.
2. Using construction paper, design a building that looks like your church building. Make sure the doors are attached so that they open and close. The building should cover the bulletin board, and can extend over the top and across the sides.
3. Staple the church design to the bulletin board. When the doors open, you will see the blank white paper underneath.
4. Take numerous photos of your congregation in various church activities (choir singing, pastor preaching, congregation worshiping, committees meeting, people visiting). You will need enough to cover the blank white paper behind the doors of the design.

Directions

1. Seat the kids where they can see the bulletin board.
2. Put the photos in a large container.

3. Let each child reach in and pull out a photo. Have them tell you what is happening in the photo. Provide hints and clues, if needed.
4. Have each child place the photo in the blank white space beneath the doors. As the child puts the picture on the board, he/she can say, "Praise God for _____ (our pastor, the choir, Sunday school teacher, and so forth)." The rest of the kids can respond with "Thanks be to God for _____ (church name)!"
5. When the bulletin board is complete, you can say:

> Here is our church.
> It's filled with God's people.
> Look! Open the doors!
> And see our great people.

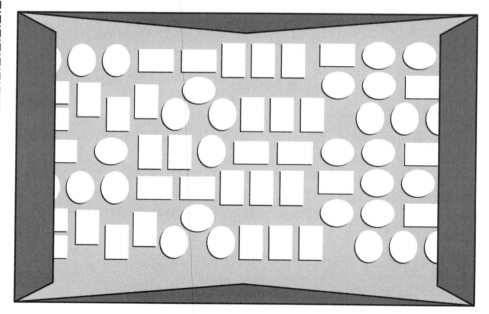

The Bulletin Board

 **GAME**

A Church Treasure Hunt

Adapt this to meet the ages and abilities of the children, and to the layout of your church. Below is a sample hunt for grades 1 and 2. Hide each item well, since kids this age love to hunt, and they are good finders!

CLUE 1: Jesus died on the _____.
(Clue 2 is hidden near the cross in the sanctuary.)

CLUE 2: We can learn about Jesus by reading the _____.
(Clue 3 is hidden in or near the Bible on the altar.)

CLUE 3: Do you know the Bible story about Creation?
(Clue 4 is hidden near the Creation window in the sanctuary.)

CLUE 4: We enjoy hearing the _____ sing for worship services.
(Clue 5 is hidden in the choir loft.)

CLUE 5: Pastor _____ stands here to share the message.
(Clue 6 is hidden in the pulpit.)

CLUE 6: This book has many songs that are fun to sing.
(Clue 7 is hidden in a hymnal. It can be sticking out, so that the kids can find it as they walk among the rows of seats.)

CLUE 7: Don't chew gum in church, but if you do, don't you dare stick it under your seat!
(Clue 8 is taped to the bottom of a chair or pew.)

CLUE 8: The ushers will pass these around. Drop your money inside!
(Clue 9 is hidden in an offering plate.)

CLUE 9: This is where we baptize people.
(Clue 10 is hidden near the baptism font.)

CLUE 10: You're great at finding your way around the sanctuary. Now see if you can find your way back to the fellowship hall, where someone has a surprise for you.

HINTS ✳

1. Use picture clues for preschool and kindergarten kids. Have parents help them.

2. Enlist adults as guides, but always let the kids figure things out on their own.

3. For grades 3 through 5, create challenging puzzles. Have them look in their Bibles to find answers. Have them complete a word puzzle that tells them where the next clue is.

4. For large groups of kids, divide them into teams of four children each. Color code each team's clues (for example, blue paper for team 1, and green paper for team 2).

5. When working with teams of children who are hunting in the same area, vary the order of the clues, and start each team three minutes after the previous team has started.

PUZZLE
How Does God Feel?

Color B=Blue, G=Green, R=Red, P=Purple, Y=Yellow

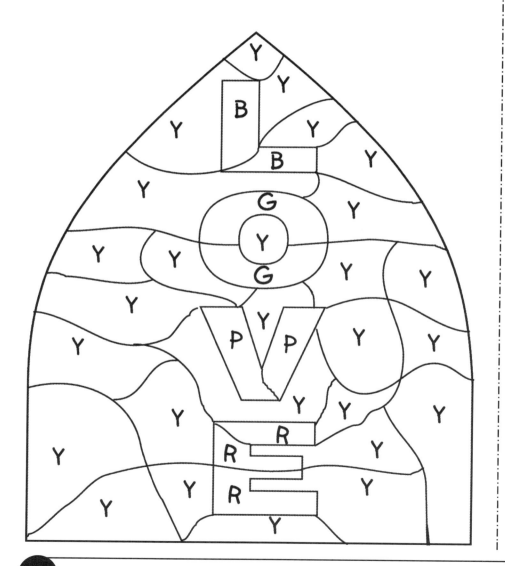

PUZZLE
What Does God Want?

Unscramble the words below. Print the circled letters in the spaces provided on the left to discover what the message is.

____ NGEACH ◯__ __ __ __ __

____ BEYO ◯__ __ __

____ SICMU ◯__ __ __ __

____ VELO __ __ __ ◯

____ RUTST __ __ __ __ ◯

____ GIVEROF __ ◯__ __ __ __ __

____ RACE ◯__ __ __

____ SHIPWOR __ __ __ __ __ ◯ __

____ GHUAL __ __ ◯__ __

____ ARESH __ __ __ ◯ __

____ HEERC ◯__ __ __ __

____ PELH ◯__ __ __

Room Decoration Ideas

Decorating for children's programs can be fun. The following suggestions will help make your programs more realistic and enjoyable for the kids. Once the decorations have been made, they can be used again and again.

1. Enlist the assistance of college, community, and high school theater departments in designing backdrops and other settings. They will know what materials to use and how best to design and construct them.

2. Use illustrations and photographs from books on ancient Bible times to help you in designing backdrops and sets. Several suggestions appear on pages 136-40. Also investigate books on stage design and scenery.

3. Create an entrance arch to your Christian education area. This should represent what you are studying. Make it portable so that it can be easily removed and placed each week, if your church shares space with a preschool or day care center. If your program uses several classrooms, make entrance arches for each of them. Give each classroom a different biblical name (for example, Jericho Junction, Gideon's Gate House, or Fisherman's Wharf).

4. Purchase white window shades and paints that will adhere to this type of surface. Ask a few of the artists in your church to design and paint biblical scenes on the shades. Choose several general locales from the Bible (Mount Sinai, Sea of Galilee, sheep pastures). After each scene is completed, let the shades dry and then roll them up. Affix permanent hardware to your wall or ceiling to hang the shades. This allows you to "change scenes" to accommodate different stories in the Bible.

5. Look for wallpaper murals that could be used for biblical scenery. They can be made into backdrops. Ask college, high school, or local theater staff to show you how.

6. Paint several large cardboard packing boxes to look like buildings. These can be set up, taken down, stored, and then reused each week. Again, ask the "theater experts" to show you how.

7. Design a biblical town, displaying buildings, carpentry benches, and various sites. Children can move from one part of the town to another as they participate in the activities.

8. Design a biblical home that is filled with artifacts a family would have used. Have kids sit on woven throw rugs as they listen to the stories.

9. Purchase large palm plants to add authenticity to your scenes.

10. Buy an inexpensive, large wooden rowboat that can be converted to a fishing boat or a sailboat. Let the kids sit in it as they lis-

ten to various Bible stories. Drape fishnets with fish in them (actual dead fish or plastic look-alikes) over the sides of the boat.

11. Make tabernacles (tents) for the kids to sit inside. Spread woven throw rugs on the floor for the kids to sit on.

12. A child's swimming pool filled with water can become a part of the Sea of Galilee or other body of water. Surround the pool with plants, large rocks, and sand to add realism.

13. Use tables that can be locked at a variety of heights. Have one table set low to the ground. Designate this as the food table and decorate it according to the story you are sharing. Put two tables that are the same height along each side. Cover them with cushions and colored cloth draped over the sides. The kids can sit on these "benches" as they dine from the table in the middle.

14. Have biblical artifacts on hand that illustrate the stories you are sharing with the kids.

15. Dress in authentic clothing as you present your programs. Take on the persona of a Bible character and relate the story from their perspective. Ask other adults in your congregation to dress up and portray actual characters or townspeople. In addition, they can assist with the program as needed.

16. Make costumes in various kid sizes, and let the children wear them. Label each costume with a child's name, and store the outfits at the church. Let the kids go barefoot or wear sandals.

17. Use audiotape and CD recordings of sound effects. Place tape or CD players out of sight of the kids.

18. Have large fans blow wind to accompany appropriate stories.

Place the fans out of sight as much as possible, so that kids cannot see them but can hear and feel the wind.

19. Create authentic-looking footpaths that wind their way through your locales. Use gray and brown paper for tiled surfaces; contact paper can be stuck to carpet.

20. Enlist the gifts and talents of members of your congregation. Some people may be unwilling to teach but may be willing to paint scenery, make costumes, build sets, or prepare foods. Let everyone help you with the children's Christian education by sharing their unique talents.

Each of the books listed below contain drawings of places, costumes, and artifacts from biblical times. They can provide useful information for room decorations and costuming.

Hastings, Selina. *The Children's Illustrated Bible.*
London: Dorling Kindersley, 1994.

Hunter, Elrose. *The Story Atlas of the Bible.*
Parsippany, N.J.: Silver Burdett Press, 1994.

Mason, Antony. *If You Were There in Biblical Times.*
New York: Simon & Schuster, 1996.

Tubb, Jonathan N. *Bible Lands.*
New York: Alfred A. Knopf, 1991.

In addition, check your library for other books about life in Bible times. "Bible—Antiquities" and "Bible—History of Biblical Events" are two subject searches that may help. Children's picture-book story Bibles also will have illustrations that can help.

Discipline Tips

You must have discipline if your programs are to run smoothly. Children will derive more enjoyment and knowledge from a program where everyone behaves appropriately. Here are some tips that will help you maintain a disciplined and positive classroom atmosphere.

1. Make sure children know exactly what behavior is expected of them. "When listening to stories, everyone must sit on the floor. Sit on your bottom, with your feet crossed under you like this. (Show them.) Fold your hands, and put them in your lap like this. (Show them.) Please listen without talking or whispering. That way everyone can enjoy the story."

2. Have a list of rules posted where all the kids can see them. ("No running. No name calling. Don't hurt others. . . .") Go over these rules with children and parents. Explain the reasons for the rules. Explain that God wants us to behave in a way that will help, not hurt, other people. Quote the Golden Rule: Treat people the way you want to be treated.

3. If parents are present, remind them that this is a time for them to participate in a program with their kids. It is not a time for them to sit off to the side or stand in the back and visit with one another.
   "Parents, you need to sit with your kids. Please set a good example by listening quietly. And, please participate in the activities along with your child."

4. Have consequences that fit the behavior. Use timeouts; remove child from a program and take the child to his/her parents; call parents to come get a child; and so forth. A child who purposely splatters paint on another person loses painting privileges.

5. If a child causes a distraction with a parent present, ask the parent to take the child out of the room for a few minutes. The child can return once he/she is ready to participate appropriately. If parents are not present, feel free to remove the child and take him/her to the parents. Explain that the child did not want to participate, and that maybe next time things will go better. Always let parents know exactly what happened so that they can discuss it with their child.

6. Children should never be allowed to make fun of, tease, or hurt another child. This kind of behavior must be stopped immediately. Explain to the child that this behavior is hurtful and wrong. Let the child's parents know what happened so that they can discuss the matter at home. Never allow anyone to say "Well, that's just how kids are." Children can be taught to treat others with kindness and respect.

7. Those of you who are child-free may have a parent say, "But you're not a parent." Respond with "But I am the adult in charge of the program, and I expect the children to behave in a respectful manner." If you have had experience working with children, add, "I work with children, and I do not allow this kind of behavior. I'd appreciate your cooperation in helping your child learn to treat adults with respect and courtesy."

8. There are some children who have serious behavior problems. Talk to your director of Christian education and your pastor to determine how you want to handle such situations. Work together with the parents (and perhaps the child's school) to devise a positive plan for working with these children.

9. Praise children: "Thank you for your cooperation. It really helps when everyone works together as well as you did today."

10. Be consistent. Follow through all the time. Inconsistency confuses children, and it is unfair. Let them know that rules must be followed all the time or there will be a consequence.

Resource List

B

Bodker, Cecil. *Mary of Nazareth.*
New York: Farrar, Straus & Giroux, 1989.
   Mary tells the story of the birth of her holy Son, Jesus.

Brenner, Barbara. *Group Soup.*
New York: Viking, 1992.
   While their mother is away, the kids have to make their own dinner of vegetable soup.

C

Chaikin, Miriam. *Children's Bible Stories from Genesis to Daniel.*
New York: Dial, 1993.
   The story of Father Abraham is retold.

——. *Make Noise, Make Merry.*
New York: Clarion Books, 1983.
   This book includes the story of Esther as well as an explanation about the holiday Purim. Also included is information about games and foods to help celebrate this feast.

Cone, Molly. *Purim.*
New York: Thomas Y. Crowell Company, 1967.
   Learn how Queen Esther saved the Jewish people, causing them to celebrate a holiday in her honor.

D

dePaola, Tomie. *The Legend of the Poinsettia.*
New York: Putnam, 1991.
   A little girl's gift of weeds turns into a beautiful flower.

——. *Mary, the Mother of Jesus.*
New York: Holiday House, 1995.
   This is a beautifully told and illustrated story of Jesus' mother, Mary.

——. *Tomie dePaola's Book of Bible Stories.*
New York: Putnam's, 1990.
   This includes an excellent retelling of the Father Abraham story.

Dingwall, Cindy. *Bible Time with Kids.*
Nashville: Abingdon Press, 1997.
   This contains enjoyable ways to present Bible stories to kids. It includes songs, games, and art.

——. *Worship Time with Kids.*
Nashville: Abingdon Press, 1998.
   A cornucopia of enjoyable worship activities to use with children.

DiSalvo-Ryan, DyAnne. *Uncle Willie and the Soup Kitchen.*
New York: Morrow Junior Books, 1991.
   Uncle Willie takes his nephew with him to work in a church soup kitchen.

Dooley, Norah. *Everybody Bakes Bread.*
Minneapolis: Carolrhoda Books, 1996.
   Carrie's mother sends her on a rainy-day errand in which she visits her neighbors and learns all about different kinds of bread. Recipes are included.

E

Ehlert, Lois. *Growing Vegetable Soup.*
San Diego: Harcourt Brace Jovanovich, 1987.
   A boy and his grandpa grow vegetables that they use to make vegetable soup.

Elkin, Benjamin. *The Wisest Man in the World.*
New York: Parents Magazine Press, 1968.
   The Queen of Sheba tests King Solomon to see just how wise he really is.

F

Fitzsimmons, Cecilia. *Fruit.*
Parsippany, N.J.: Silver Burdett, 1997.
   This fascinating book tells about fruits and where they grow. It includes a variety of interesting fruit-related activities and recipes.

G

Gauch, Patricia Lee. *Christina Katerina and Fats and the Great Neighborhood War.*
New York: Putnam, 1997.
   The kids who had always been such good friends are now at war with one another.

Gershator, David and Phillis. *Bread Is for Eating.*
New York: Henry Holt & Company, 1995.
   A mother explains the importance of bread through story and song.

Giblin, James Cross. *Fireworks, Picnics, and Flags.*
New York: Clarion Books, 1983.
   This book is bursting with fascinating stories and facts about the Fourth of July.

Goodman, Naomi. *The Good Book Cookbook: Recipes from Biblical Times.*
New York: Dodd & Mead Company, 1986.

Graham-Barber, Lynda. *Doodle Dandy! The Complete Book of Independence Day Words.*
New York: Bradbury Press, 1992.
   Amusing games, facts, and fun fill this fascinating book of Fourth of July fun.

———. *Great People of the Bible and How They Lived.*
Pleasantville, N.Y.: Reader's Digest Association Inc., 1974.
   This book provides outstanding information about biblical times and people.

Guthrie, Woody. *This Land Is Your Land.*
Boston: Little, Brown & Company, 1998.
   This beautifully illustrated book of the song includes music and lyrics.

H

Haidle, Helen and David. *The Candymaker's Gift.*
Tulsa, Okla.: Honor Books, 1996.
   A candymaker makes a candy cane that tells about Jesus.

Harbison, Elizabeth M. *Loaves of Fun.*
Chicago: Chicago Review Press, 1997.
   This outstanding book presents the history of bread throughout the world. It is accompanied by recipes and crafts.

Hastings, Selina. *The Children's Illustrated Bible.*
London: Dorling Kindersley, 1994.
    Excellent source of illustrations and information about how things were in Bible times.

Hilton, Nette. *Andrew Jessup.*
New York: Ticknor & Fields, 1993.
    Andrew's best friend has moved away, but soon a new friend moves in next door.

Hines, Anna Grossnickle. *Daddy Makes the Best Spaghetti.*
New York: Clarion Books, 1986.
    Daddy does make the best spaghetti.

Hunt, Angela Elwell. *The Tale of Three Trees.*
Batavia, Ill.: Lion Publishing, 1989.
    Each of the three trees has a special purpose in life.

Hunter, Elrose. *The Story Atlas of the Bible.*
Parsippany, N.J.: Silver Burdett Press, 1994.
    Maps and illustrations provide good information for planning Bible-based programs.

I

Icks, Marguerite. *The Book of Religious Holidays and Celebrations.*
New York: Dodd, Mead & Company, 1966.
    This book is filled with important information about religious celebrations.

J

Jones, Judith, et al. *Knead It, Punch It, Bake It!*
Boston: Houghton Mifflin, 1998.
    This breadmaking book is for parents and kids.

Joose, Barbara. *Mama, Do You Love Me?*
San Francisco: Chronicles Books, 1991.
    A mother reassures her child of how much love a mother has for a child.

K

Kyrthe, Maymie. *All About American Holidays.*
New York: Harper & Row Publishers, 1962.
    Many of our religious holidays are explained.

M

Mason, Antony. *If You Were There in Biblical Times.*
New York: Simon & Schuster, 1996.
    A wealth of illustrations provides much information for sharing biblical activities with children.

McDonnell, Janet. *Fourth of July.*
Chicago, Ill. Children's Press, 1994.
    Nina and her dog have a wonderful Fourth of July surprise.

Mitgutsh, Ali. *From Fruit to Jam.*
Minneapolis: Carolrhoda Books, 1991.
    Learn how fruit becomes jam.

Mormon Tabernacle Choir. "God Bless America."
New York: Sony Masterworks, 1992.
    This recording includes "America the Beautiful," "God Bless America," "This Is My Country," "You're a Grand Old Flag," and many more patriotic songs. Let everyone sing with the recording.

Morris, Ann. *Bread, Bread, Bread.*
New York: Lothrop, Lee & Shepard Books, 1989.
   Enjoy celebrating with people all over the world as they enjoy different kinds of bread.

N

Nelson, Gertrude Mueller. *To Dance with God.*
Mahwah, N.J.: Paulist Press, 1986.
   This book is filled with ideas for joyous holiday celebrations.

O

Orgel, Doris. *Button Soup.*
New York: Bantam, 1994.
   A poor woman convinces everyone in the neighborhood to help her make button soup.

———. *The Flower of Sheba.*
New York: Bantam Books, 1994.
   A bee helps King Solomon pass a rather tricky test.

P

Parker, Kristy. *My Dad Is Magnificent.*
New York: Dutton, 1987.
   A boy tells his friend about all the great things his dad does.

Patterson, Geoffrey. *All About Bread.*
London: Andre Deutsch, 1984.
   Learn about the history of bread from prehistoric times to the present. This book tells how wheat is grown, ground into flower, and made into bread.

Pfister, Marcus. *The Christmas Star.*
New York: North-South Books, 1993.
   The shepherds and some wise men follow a bright star to find a baby who is King.

———. *The Rainbow Fish.*
New York: North-South Books, 1992.
   Rainbow Fish learns an important lesson about making friends and sharing what he has.

———. *Rainbow Fish to the Rescue.*
New York: North-South Books, 1995.
   Rainbow Fish decides to befriend the new striped fish who has moved in.

Pienkowski, Jan. *Easter.*
New York: Knopf, 1989.
   The Easter story is told and illustrated for children.

Polushkin, Maria. *Mother, Mother, I Want Another.*
New York: Crown Publishers, 1978.
   A boy refuses to go to sleep until his mother gives him another goodnight kiss.

Porter, Laurel Gaylad. *I Love My Mommy Because.*
New York: Dutton Children's Books, 1991.
   A child tells all the reasons for loving Mom.

Powers, Mala. *Follow the Year: A Family Celebration of Christian Holidays.*
San Francisco: Harper & Row Publishers, 1985.
   This book outlines many enjoyable things families can do to celebrate holidays.

R

Renberg, Dalia Hardof. *King Solomon and the Bee.*
New York: HarperCollins, 1994.
   The Queen of Sheba devises a riddle to trick King Solomon. However, a crafty bee helps King Solomon answer the riddle.

Robinson, Fay. *We Love Fruit.*
Chicago: Children's Press, 1992.
    It is interesting to learn about fruits and to watch them grow.

S

Silverman, Maida. *The Festival of Esther: The Story of Purim.*
New York: Simon & Schuster, 1989.
    Here is the story of Queen Esther and the holiday of Purim.

Skarmeas, Nancy and Fran Morley, eds. *An American Thanksgiving.*
Nashville: Ideals Publishing Corporation, 1991.
    This book is brimming with Thanksgiving ideas.

Smith, Jeff. *The Frugal Gourmet Keeps the Feast: Past, Present, and Future.*
New York: William Morrow & Company, 1995.
    The Frugal Gourmet provides facts and ideas for religious holiday celebrations.

T

Teringo, J. Robert. *The Land and People Jesus Knew.*
Minneapolis: Bethany House Publishers, 1985.
    Filled with information, this book provides an interesting look at life in biblical times.

Turner, Dorothy. *Bread.*
Minneapolis: Carolrhoda Books, 1989.
    Find out how bread is produced, prepared, and eaten. Two bread recipes are included.

U

The United Methodist Hymnal.
Nashville: United Methodist Publishing House, 1989.
    This hymnal includes "America the Beautiful"; "Blest Be the Tie That Binds"; "Eat This Bread"; "Let Us Break Bread Together"; "One Bread, One Body"; "We Are the Church"; and "We Gather Together."

W

Waddell, Martin. *Stories from the Bible: Old Testament Stories Retold.*
New York: Ticknor & Fields, 1993.
    A good retelling about Abraham and his family.

Walburg, Lori. *The Legend of the Candy Cane.*
Grand Rapids: Zondervan, 1997.
    Lucy is entranced to learn the story of the candy cane when she helps Mr. Sonneman in his candy store.

Wolf, Jake. *Daddy, Could I Have an Elephant?*
New York: Greenwillow Books, 1996.
    A child tries to talk his dad into buying a pet.

Z

Zolotow, Charlotte. *The Song.*
New York: Greenwillow Books, 1982.
    A young girl hears a special song that no one else can hear. One day she meets a little boy who can hear it too.

EES
SEE

I

MA
A M

KINGAM
MAKING

LAL
ALL

NIGTSH
THINGS

EWN
NEW

NOLATEREVI
REVELATION 21:5

A Parade of Love   Page 16

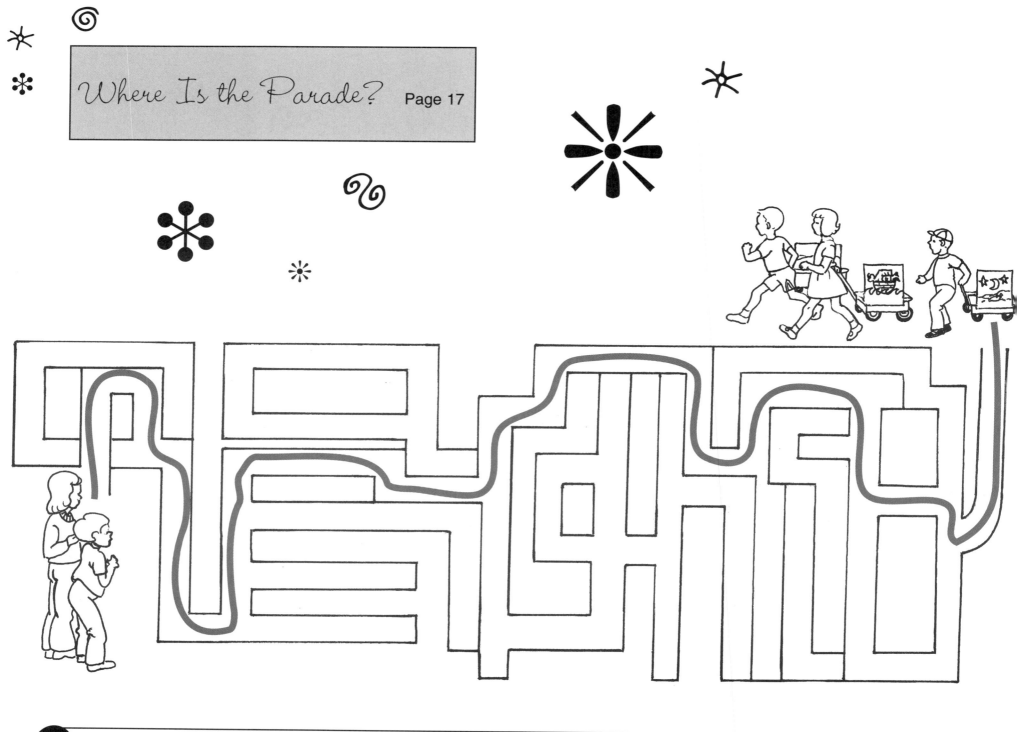

Where Is the Parade?   Page 17

Where Is Jesus?   Page 22

SHARE YOUR GIFTS

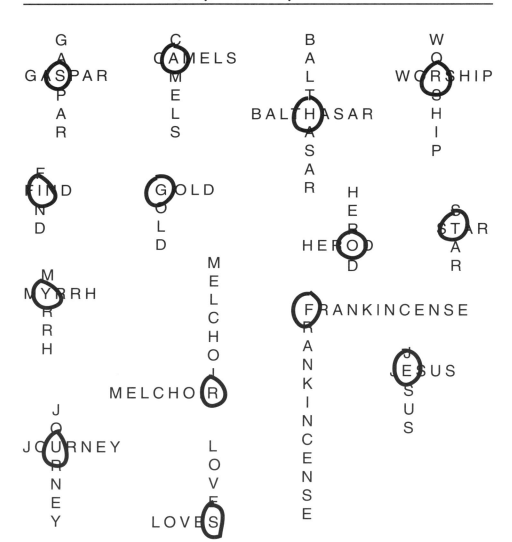

G
A
GASPAR
P
A
R

C
CAMELS
M
E
L
S

B
A
L
BALTHASAR
A
S
A
R

W
WORSHIP
R
S
H
I
P

F
FIND
N
D

G
GOLD
L
D

H
E
R
HEROD
D

S
STAR
A
R

M
MYRRH
R
H

M
E
L
C
H
MELCHOIR
R

F
FRANKINCENSE
A
N
K
I
N
C
E
N
S
E

J
JESUS
S
U
S

J
O
JOURNEY
R
N
E
Y

L
O
V
LOVES

Message from
the Wise Men   Page 22

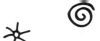

Word search solution in bowl:

CARROTS BAYLEAVES
CELERY SNOODLES
POTATOESCHICKENWATER
CHICKEN ONIONS
BOUILLONCUBES

SHARE
SOUP!

Soup's On! Page 27

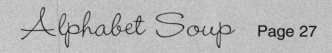

BIBLE BANQUETS WITH KIDS

LET US LOVE

ONE ANOTHER

DEAR FRIENDS

SHARE IT

S E J U S
<u>J</u> <u>E</u> <u>(S)</u> <u>U</u> <u>S</u>

H I S F
<u>F</u> <u>I</u> <u>S</u> <u>(H)</u>

T E A
<u>E</u> <u>(A)</u> <u>T</u>

D R E B A
<u>B</u> <u>(R)</u> <u>E</u> <u>A</u> <u>D</u>

L S O E A V
<u>L</u> <u>O</u> <u>A</u> <u>V</u> <u>(E)</u> <u>S</u>

S E L C I P I S D
<u>D</u> <u>(I)</u> <u>S</u> <u>C</u> <u>I</u> <u>P</u> <u>L</u> <u>E</u> <u>S</u>

T U D E M U L T I
<u>M</u> <u>U</u> <u>L</u> <u>(T)</u> <u>I</u> <u>T</u> <u>U</u> <u>D</u> <u>E</u>

More Than Enough Page 40

A Brave Queen   Page 45

QUEEN ESTHER SAVED
HER PEOPLE.

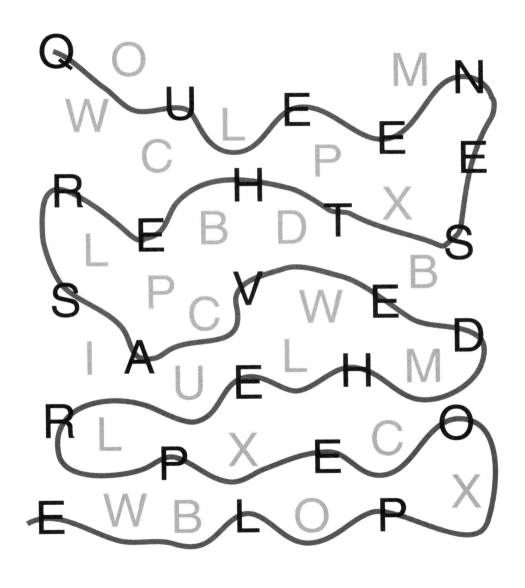

FINISH!

START

Where's the Banquet Hall?
Page 45

Puzzle grid:

J	L	O	V	E					
M	E	E	H	S					
Y	E	S	O	Y					
G	O	U	P	O					
S	L	A	L	O	R	D	E	U	B	A	B	Y
W	O	W	L	B	E	T	H	L	E	H	E	M
I	J	E	S	U	S	S	A	V	I	O	R	Y
A	N	G	E	L	U	D	C	R	O	S	S	V
		E	R	I	N	P					
		M	R	S	A	R					
		I	E	C	Z	A					
		R	C	I	A	Y					
		A	T	P	R	E					
		C	I	L	E	R					
		L	O	E	T	S					
		E	N	S	H	S					

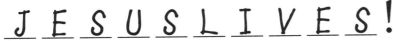

J E S U S L I V E S !

Which two words are listed twice?

GO & MY

F I G S
A
P A P A Y A → P E A C H E S
→ L E M O N S
A
C → G R A P E F R U I T
S T R A W B E R R I E S
→ P L U M S
B A N A N A S
H O N E Y D E W
D A T E S
N E C T A R I N E S

GOD CREATED
1 2 3 4 5 6 7 8 9 10

TASTY FRUITS!
11 12 13 14 15 16 17 18 19 20 21

BIBLE BANQUETS WITH KIDS

What Do Moms Do All Day? Page 62

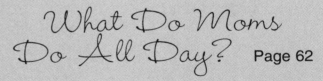

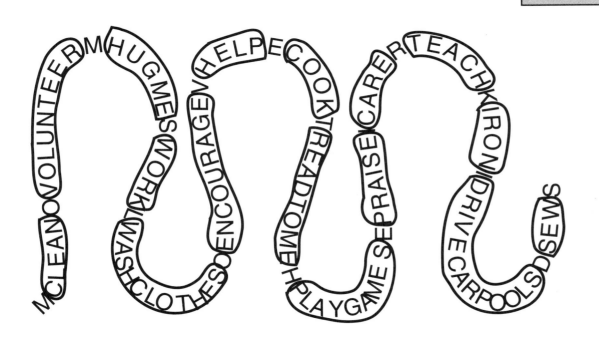

MCLEAN VOLUNTEER M HUGMES WORK WASHCLOTHES ENCOURAGE HELPE COOK READTOME PLAYGAME PRAISE CARER TEACH IRON DRIVE CARPOOLS SEWS

MOMS LOVE
THEIR KIDS!

What Is God Trying to Tell Us?   Page 68

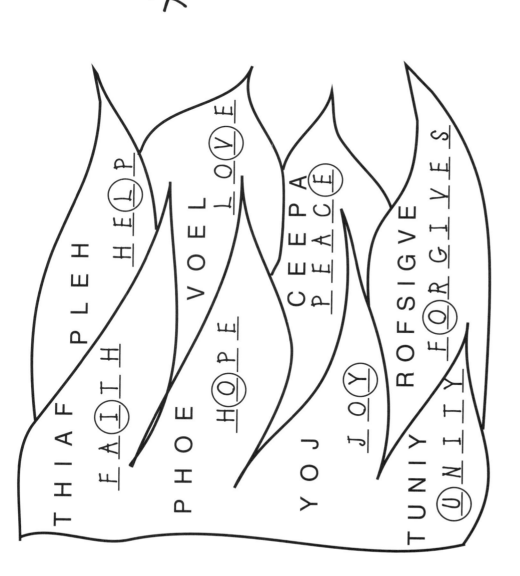

THIAF PLEH   H E L P
F A (I) T H

PHOE VOEL   L (O) V E
H (O) P E

CEEPA   P E A C (E)
J O (Y)

ROFSIGVE   F (O) R G I V E S
TUNIY   (U) N I T Y

I LOVE YOU

What Do You See
in the Flames?   Page 68

DAD LOVES ME!

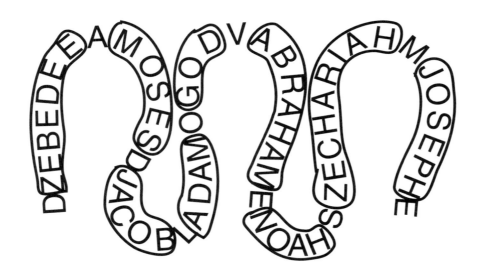

Who's Who? Page 75

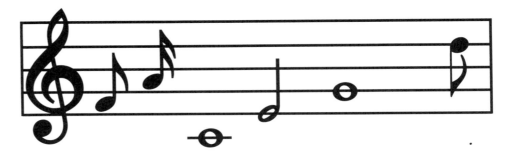

FACE GOD

FOR GRACE

Where Do We Go?   Page 81

Finish

Choir Practice

Come Sing With Us

Start

Write it here: __P__ __E__ __A__ __C__ __E__.

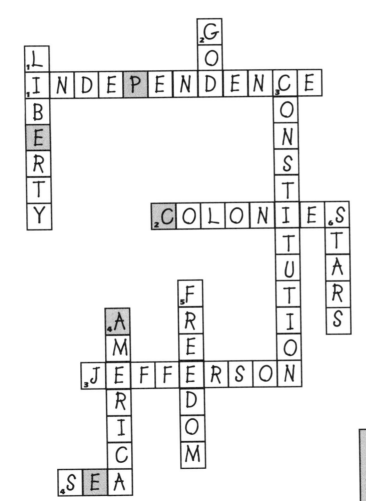

ACROSS:
1. The Declaration of ____Independence____.
2. There were thirteen ____Colonies____ that formed the United States.
3. Thomas ____Jefferson____ helped write the Constitution
4. From __sea__ to shining sea.

DOWN:
1. Sweet land of __Liberty__.
2. In __God__ we trust.
3. The ____Constitution____ is the document that governs the United States of America.
4. ____America____ the beautiful.
5. In the United States, we have ____Freedom____ of religion.
6. There are fifty __Stars__ on our flag.

America the Beautiful **Page 86**

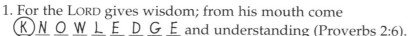

1. For the LORD gives wisdom; from his mouth come (K)N O W L E D G E and understanding (Proverbs 2:6).
2. Trust in the LORD with all your heart, and do not rely on your own I N S (I) G H T (Proverbs 3:5).
3. My child, do not forget your teaching, but let your heart keep my C O M M A N D M E (N) T S (Proverbs 3:1).
4. Hear instruction and be wise, and do not N E (G) L E C T it (Proverbs 8:33).
5. A W I (S) E child loves discipline, but a scoffer does not listen to rebuke (Proverbs 13:1).
6. A soft answer turns away wrath, but a harsh W (O) R D stirs up anger (Proverbs 15:1).
7. The eyes of the (L) O R D are in every place, keeping watch on the evil and the good (Proverbs 15:3).
8. The light of the eyes R E J (O) I C E S the heart, and the good news refreshes the body (Proverbs 15:30).
9. C O M (M) I T your work to the LORD, and your plans will be established (Proverbs 16:3).
10. The human mind plans the way, but the L (O) R D directs the steps (Proverbs 16:9).
11. The (N) A M E of the LORD is a strong tower; the righteous run into it and are safe (Proverbs 18:10).
12. To (W) A T C H over mouth and tongue is to keep out of trouble (Proverbs 21:23).
13. Apply your mind to instruction and your E (A) R to words of knowledge (Proverbs 23:12).
14. My child, give me your heart, and let your E Y E (S) observe my ways (Proverbs 23:26).
15. Every (W) O R D of God proves true; he is a shield to those who take refuge in him (Proverbs 30:5).
16. Listen, C H (I) L D R E N, to a father's instruction, and be attentive, that you may gain insight (Proverbs 4:1).
17. Lying lips are an abomination to the LORD, but T H (O) S E who act faithfully are his delight (Proverbs 12:22).
18. Whoever walks with the W I S (E) becomes wise (Proverbs 13:20a).

Print the circled letters here. What's the message?

K I N G   S O L O M O N   W A S   W I S E.

Wisdom Page 91

World Wide Communion
Sunday   Page 96

G O D   L O V E S
7   15   4   12   15   22   5   19

K I D S   A L L
11   9   4   19   1   12   12

O V E R   T H E
15   22   5   18   20   8   5

W O R L D
23   15   18   12   4

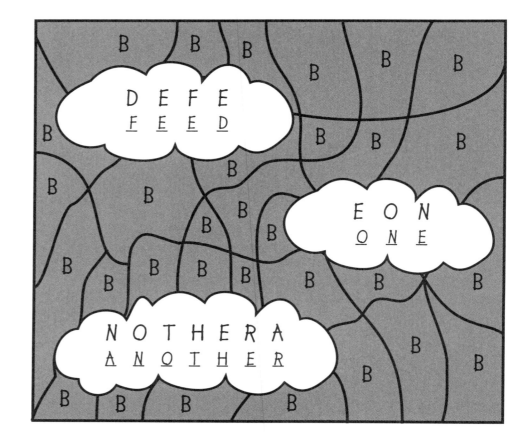

DEFE
_F_ _E_ _E_ _D_

EON
_O_ _N_ _E_

NOTHERA
_A_ _N_ _O_ _T_ _H_ _E_ _R_

What Should We Do? Page 103

BIBLE BANQUETS WITH KIDS

How Can We Help?   Page 103

Thanksgiving Message   Page 111

X	G	X	X	X	X	X	X	I	X	X	
X	V	X	X	E	X	X	X	T	X	X	H
X	X	A	X	N	X	X	X	K	X	X	X
S	X	X	T	X	X	O	X	T	X	X	X
X	X	H	X	X	E	X	X	X	X	X	L
X	O	X	X	R	X	D	X	X	X	F	X
X	X	O	X	X	R	X	X	G	X	X	O
X	X	D	X	X	I	X	S	X	X	G	
	X	X	O	X	O	X	D	X	X		

G I V E T H A N K S T O T H E
L O R D F O R G O D I S
G O O D !

Look in your Bible. What psalm is this from?

PSALM 106:1

S T A R

P O I N S E T T I A

C H R I S T M A S T R E E

What do the circled letters spell?

CHRISTMAS

C A N D Y C A N E

B E L L S

H O L L Y

C A N D L E

W R E A T H

A N G E L S

Christmas   Page 118

Going to Church   Page 125

HAPPY BIRTHDAY

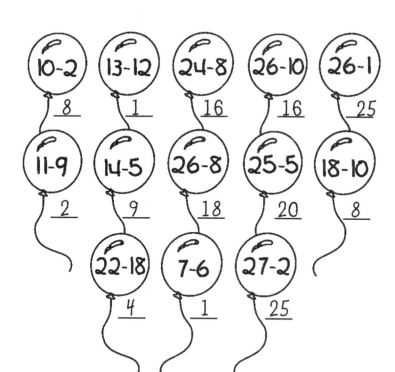

C NGEACH (C) H A N G E

O BEYO (O) B E Y

M SICMU (M) U S I C

E VELO L O V (E)

T RUTST T R U S (T)

O GIVEROF F (O) R G I V E

C RACE (C) A R E

H SHIPWOR W O R S (H) I P

U GHUAL L A (U) G H

R ARESH S H A (R) E

C HEERC (C) H E E R

H PELH (H) E L P

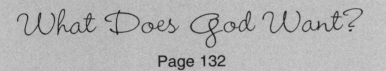

What Does God Want?

Page 132

INDEX

Scripture Index

Title and Topic Index

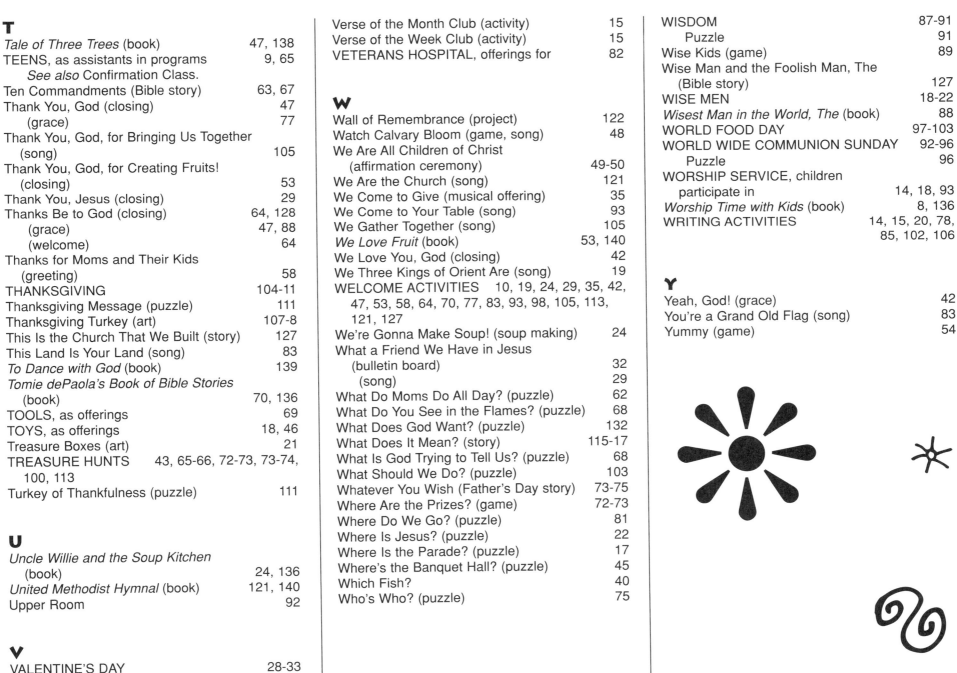